Mometrix TEST PREPARATION

AP®

Microeconomics Exam Secrets Study Guide

DEAR FUTURE EXAM SUCCESS STORY

First of all, **THANK YOU** for purchasing Mometrix study materials!

Second, congratulations! You are one of the few determined test-takers who are committed to doing whatever it takes to excel on your exam. **You have come to the right place.** We developed these study materials with one goal in mind: to deliver you the information you need in a format that's concise and easy to use.

In addition to optimizing your guide for the content of the test, we've outlined our recommended steps for breaking down the preparation process into small, attainable goals so you can make sure you stay on track.

We've also analyzed the entire test-taking process, identifying the most common pitfalls and showing how you can overcome them and be ready for any curveball the test throws you.

Standardized testing is one of the biggest obstacles on your road to success, which only increases the importance of doing well in the high-pressure, high-stakes environment of test day. Your results on this test could have a significant impact on your future, and this guide provides the information and practical advice to help you achieve your full potential on test day.

Your success is our success

We would love to hear from you! If you would like to share the story of your exam success or if you have any questions or comments in regard to our products, please contact us at **800-673-8175** or **support@mometrix.com**.

Thanks again for your business and we wish you continued success!

Sincerely,
The Mometrix Test Preparation Team

Need more help? Check out our flashcards at:
http://MometrixFlashcards.com/AP

TABLE OF CONTENTS

Introduction

Thank you for purchasing this resource! You have made the choice to prepare yourself for a test that could have a huge impact on your future, and this guide is designed to help you be fully ready for test day. Obviously, it's important to have a solid understanding of the test material, but you also need to be prepared for the unique environment and stressors of the test, so that you can perform to the best of your abilities.

For this purpose, the first section that appears in this guide is the **Secret Keys**. We've devoted countless hours to meticulously researching what works and what doesn't, and we've boiled down our findings to the five most impactful steps you can take to improve your performance on the test. We start at the beginning with study planning and move through the preparation process, all the way to the testing strategies that will help you get the most out of what you know when you're finally sitting in front of the test.

We recommend that you start preparing for your test as far in advance as possible. However, if you've bought this guide as a last-minute study resource and only have a few days before your test, we recommend that you skip over the first two Secret Keys since they address a long-term study plan.

If you struggle with **test anxiety**, we strongly encourage you to check out our recommendations for how you can overcome it. Test anxiety is a formidable foe, but it can be beaten, and we want to make sure you have the tools you need to defeat it.

Secret Key #1 – Plan Big, Study Small

There's a lot riding on your performance. If you want to ace this test, you're going to need to keep your skills sharp and the material fresh in your mind. You need a plan that lets you review everything you need to know while still fitting in your schedule. We'll break this strategy down into three categories.

Information Organization

Start with the information you already have: the official test outline. From this, you can make a complete list of all the concepts you need to cover before the test. Organize these concepts into groups that can be studied together, and create a list of any related vocabulary you need to learn so you can brush up on any difficult terms. You'll want to keep this vocabulary list handy once you actually start studying since you may need to add to it along the way.

Time Management

Once you have your set of study concepts, decide how to spread them out over the time you have left before the test. Break your study plan into small, clear goals so you have a manageable task for each day and know exactly what you're doing. Then just focus on one small step at a time. When you manage your time this way, you don't need to spend hours at a time studying. Studying a small block of content for a short period each day helps you retain information better and avoid stressing over how much you have left to do. You can relax knowing that you have a plan to cover everything in time. In order for this strategy to be effective though, you have to start studying early and stick to your schedule. Avoid the exhaustion and futility that comes from last-minute cramming!

Study Environment

The environment you study in has a big impact on your learning. Studying in a coffee shop, while probably more enjoyable, is not likely to be as fruitful as studying in a quiet room. It's important to keep distractions to a minimum. You're only planning to study for a short block of time, so make the most of it. Don't pause to check your phone or get up to find a snack. It's also important to **avoid multitasking**. Research has consistently shown that multitasking will make your studying dramatically less effective. Your study area should also be comfortable and well-lit so you don't have the distraction of straining your eyes or sitting on an uncomfortable chair.

The time of day you study is also important. You want to be rested and alert. Don't wait until just before bedtime. Study when you'll be most likely to comprehend and remember. Even better, if you know what time of day your test will be, set that time aside for study. That way your brain will be used to working on that subject at that specific time and you'll have a better chance of recalling information.

Finally, it can be helpful to team up with others who are studying for the same test. Your actual studying should be done in as isolated an environment as possible, but the work of organizing the information and setting up the study plan can be divided up. In between study sessions, you can discuss with your teammates the concepts that you're all studying and quiz each other on the details. Just be sure that your teammates are as serious about the test as you are. If you find that your study time is being replaced with social time, you might need to find a new team.

Secret Key #2 – Make Your Studying Count

You're devoting a lot of time and effort to preparing for this test, so you want to be absolutely certain it will pay off. This means doing more than just reading the content and hoping you can remember it on test day. It's important to make every minute of study count. There are two main areas you can focus on to make your studying count.

Retention

It doesn't matter how much time you study if you can't remember the material. You need to make sure you are retaining the concepts. To check your retention of the information you're learning, try recalling it at later times with minimal prompting. Try carrying around flashcards and glance at one or two from time to time or ask a friend who's also studying for the test to quiz you.

To enhance your retention, look for ways to put the information into practice so that you can apply it rather than simply recalling it. If you're using the information in practical ways, it will be much easier to remember. Similarly, it helps to solidify a concept in your mind if you're not only reading it to yourself but also explaining it to someone else. Ask a friend to let you teach them about a concept you're a little shaky on (or speak aloud to an imaginary audience if necessary). As you try to summarize, define, give examples, and answer your friend's questions, you'll understand the concepts better and they will stay with you longer. Finally, step back for a big picture view and ask yourself how each piece of information fits with the whole subject. When you link the different concepts together and see them working together as a whole, it's easier to remember the individual components.

Finally, practice showing your work on any multi-step problems, even if you're just studying. Writing out each step you take to solve a problem will help solidify the process in your mind, and you'll be more likely to remember it during the test.

Modality

Modality simply refers to the means or method by which you study. Choosing a study modality that fits your own individual learning style is crucial. No two people learn best in exactly the same way, so it's important to know your strengths and use them to your advantage.

For example, if you learn best by visualization, focus on visualizing a concept in your mind and draw an image or a diagram. Try color-coding your notes, illustrating them, or creating symbols that will trigger your mind to recall a learned concept. If you learn best by hearing or discussing information, find a study partner who learns the same way or read aloud to yourself. Think about how to put the information in your own words. Imagine that you are giving a lecture on the topic and record yourself so you can listen to it later.

For any learning style, flashcards can be helpful. Organize the information so you can take advantage of spare moments to review. Underline key words or phrases. Use different colors for different categories. Mnemonic devices (such as creating a short list in which every item starts with the same letter) can also help with retention. Find what works best for you and use it to store the information in your mind most effectively and easily.

Secret Key #3 – Practice the Right Way

Your success on test day depends not only on how many hours you put into preparing, but also on whether you prepared the right way. It's good to check along the way to see if your studying is paying off. One of the most effective ways to do this is by taking practice tests to evaluate your progress. Practice tests are useful because they show exactly where you need to improve. Every time you take a practice test, pay special attention to these three groups of questions:

- The questions you got wrong
- The questions you had to guess on, even if you guessed right
- The questions you found difficult or slow to work through

This will show you exactly what your weak areas are, and where you need to devote more study time. Ask yourself why each of these questions gave you trouble. Was it because you didn't understand the material? Was it because you didn't remember the vocabulary? Do you need more repetitions on this type of question to build speed and confidence? Dig into those questions and figure out how you can strengthen your weak areas as you go back to review the material.

Additionally, many practice tests have a section explaining the answer choices. It can be tempting to read the explanation and think that you now have a good understanding of the concept. However, an explanation likely only covers part of the question's broader context. Even if the explanation makes perfect sense, **go back and investigate** every concept related to the question until you're positive you have a thorough understanding.

As you go along, keep in mind that the practice test is just that: practice. Memorizing these questions and answers will not be very helpful on the actual test because it is unlikely to have any of the same exact questions. If you only know the right answers to the sample questions, you won't be prepared for the real thing. **Study the concepts** until you understand them fully, and then you'll be able to answer any question that shows up on the test.

It's important to wait on the practice tests until you're ready. If you take a test on your first day of study, you may be overwhelmed by the amount of material covered and how much you need to learn. Work up to it gradually.

On test day, you'll need to be prepared for answering questions, managing your time, and using the test-taking strategies you've learned. It's a lot to balance, like a mental marathon that will have a big impact on your future. Like training for a marathon, you'll need to start slowly and work your way up. When test day arrives, you'll be ready.

Start with the strategies you've read in the first two Secret Keys—plan your course and study in the way that works best for you. If you have time, consider using multiple study resources to get different approaches to the same concepts. It can be helpful to see difficult concepts from more than one angle. Then find a good source for practice tests. Many times, the test website will suggest potential study resources or provide sample tests.

Practice Test Strategy

If you're able to find at least three practice tests, we recommend this strategy:

Untimed and Open-Book Practice

Take the first test with no time constraints and with your notes and study guide handy. Take your time and focus on applying the strategies you've learned.

Timed and Open-Book Practice

Take the second practice test open-book as well, but set a timer and practice pacing yourself to finish in time.

Timed and Closed-Book Practice

Take any other practice tests as if it were test day. Set a timer and put away your study materials. Sit at a table or desk in a quiet room, imagine yourself at the testing center, and answer questions as quickly and accurately as possible.

Keep repeating timed and closed-book tests on a regular basis until you run out of practice tests or it's time for the actual test. Your mind will be ready for the schedule and stress of test day, and you'll be able to focus on recalling the material you've learned.

Secret Key #4 – Pace Yourself

Once you're fully prepared for the material on the test, your biggest challenge on test day will be managing your time. Just knowing that the clock is ticking can make you panic even if you have plenty of time left. Work on pacing yourself so you can build confidence against the time constraints of the exam. Pacing is a difficult skill to master, especially in a high-pressure environment, so **practice is vital**.

Set time expectations for your pace based on how much time is available. For example, if a section has 60 questions and the time limit is 30 minutes, you know you have to average 30 seconds or less per question in order to answer them all. Although 30 seconds is the hard limit, set 25 seconds per question as your goal, so you reserve extra time to spend on harder questions. When you budget extra time for the harder questions, you no longer have any reason to stress when those questions take longer to answer.

Don't let this time expectation distract you from working through the test at a calm, steady pace, but keep it in mind so you don't spend too much time on any one question. Recognize that taking extra time on one question you don't understand may keep you from answering two that you do understand later in the test. If your time limit for a question is up and you're still not sure of the answer, mark it and move on, and come back to it later if the time and the test format allow. If the testing format doesn't allow you to return to earlier questions, just make an educated guess; then put it out of your mind and move on.

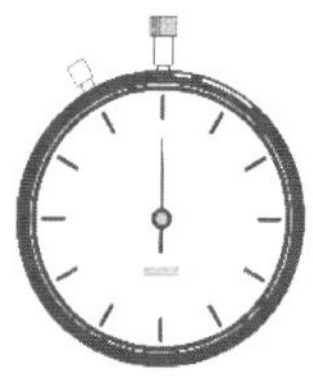

On the easier questions, be careful not to rush. It may seem wise to hurry through them so you have more time for the challenging ones, but it's not worth missing one if you know the concept and just didn't take the time to read the question fully. Work efficiently but make sure you understand the question and have looked at all of the answer choices, since more than one may seem right at first.

Even if you're paying attention to the time, you may find yourself a little behind at some point. You should speed up to get back on track, but do so wisely. Don't panic; just take a few seconds less on each question until you're caught up. Don't guess without thinking, but do look through the answer choices and eliminate any you know are wrong. If you can get down to two choices, it is often worthwhile to guess from those. Once you've chosen an answer, move on and don't dwell on any that you skipped or had to hurry through. If a question was taking too long, chances are it was one of the harder ones, so you weren't as likely to get it right anyway.

On the other hand, if you find yourself getting ahead of schedule, it may be beneficial to slow down a little. The more quickly you work, the more likely you are to make a careless mistake that will affect your score. You've budgeted time for each question, so don't be afraid to spend that time. Practice an efficient but careful pace to get the most out of the time you have.

Secret Key #5 – Have a Plan for Guessing

When you're taking the test, you may find yourself stuck on a question. Some of the answer choices seem better than others, but you don't see the one answer choice that is obviously correct. What do you do?

The scenario described above is very common, yet most test takers have not effectively prepared for it. Developing and practicing a plan for guessing may be one of the single most effective uses of your time as you get ready for the exam.

In developing your plan for guessing, there are three questions to address:

- When should you start the guessing process?
- How should you narrow down the choices?
- Which answer should you choose?

When to Start the Guessing Process

Unless your plan for guessing is to select C every time (which, despite its merits, is not what we recommend), you need to leave yourself enough time to apply your answer elimination strategies. Since you have a limited amount of time for each question, that means that if you're going to give yourself the best shot at guessing correctly, you have to decide quickly whether or not you will guess.

Of course, the best-case scenario is that you don't have to guess at all, so first, see if you can answer the question based on your knowledge of the subject and basic reasoning skills. Focus on the key words in the question and try to jog your memory of related topics. Give yourself a chance to bring the knowledge to mind, but once you realize that you don't have (or you can't access) the knowledge you need to answer the question, it's time to start the guessing process.

It's almost always better to start the guessing process too early than too late. It only takes a few seconds to remember something and answer the question from knowledge. Carefully eliminating wrong answer choices takes longer. Plus, going through the process of eliminating answer choices can actually help jog your memory.

Summary: Start the guessing process as soon as you decide that you can't answer the question based on your knowledge.

How to Narrow Down the Choices

The next chapter in this book (**Test-Taking Strategies**) includes a wide range of strategies for how to approach questions and how to look for answer choices to eliminate. You will definitely want to read those carefully, practice them, and figure out which ones work best for you. Here though, we're going to address a mindset rather than a particular strategy.

Your odds of guessing an answer correctly depend on how many options you are choosing from.

Number of options left	5	4	3	2	1
Odds of guessing correctly	20%	25%	33%	50%	100%

You can see from this chart just how valuable it is to be able to eliminate incorrect answers and make an educated guess, but there are two things that many test takers do that cause them to miss out on the benefits of guessing:

- Accidentally eliminating the correct answer
- Selecting an answer based on an impression

We'll look at the first one here, and the second one in the next section.

To avoid accidentally eliminating the correct answer, we recommend a thought exercise called **the $5 challenge**. In this challenge, you only eliminate an answer choice from contention if you are willing to bet $5 on it being wrong. Why $5? Five dollars is a small but not insignificant amount of money. It's an amount you could afford to lose but wouldn't want to throw away. And while losing $5 once might not hurt too much, doing it twenty times will set you back $100. In the same way, each small decision you make—eliminating a choice here, guessing on a question there—won't by itself impact your score very much, but when you put them all together, they can make a big difference. By holding each answer choice elimination decision to a higher standard, you can reduce the risk of accidentally eliminating the correct answer.

The $5 challenge can also be applied in a positive sense: If you are willing to bet $5 that an answer choice *is* correct, go ahead and mark it as correct.

Summary: Only eliminate an answer choice if you are willing to bet $5 that it is wrong.

Which Answer to Choose

You're taking the test. You've run into a hard question and decided you'll have to guess. You've eliminated all the answer choices you're willing to bet $5 on. Now you have to pick an answer. Why do we even need to talk about this? Why can't you just pick whichever one you feel like when the time comes?

The answer to these questions is that if you don't come into the test with a plan, you'll rely on your impression to select an answer choice, and if you do that, you risk falling into a trap. The test writers know that everyone who takes their test will be guessing on some of the questions, so they intentionally write wrong answer choices to seem plausible. You still have to pick an answer though, and if the wrong answer choices are designed to look right, how can you ever be sure that you're not falling for their trap? The best solution we've found to this dilemma is to take the decision out of your hands entirely. Here is the process we recommend:

Once you've eliminated any choices that you are confident (willing to bet $5) are wrong, select the first remaining choice as your answer.

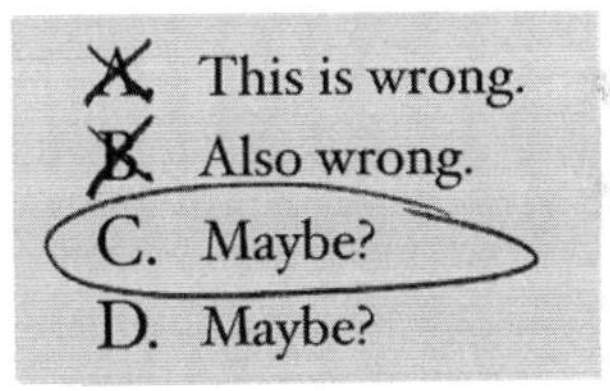

Whether you choose to select the first remaining choice, the second, or the last, the important thing is that you use some preselected standard. Using this approach guarantees that you will not be enticed into selecting an answer choice that looks right, because you are not basing your decision on how the answer choices look.

This is not meant to make you question your knowledge. Instead, it is to help you recognize the difference between your knowledge and your impressions. There's a huge difference between thinking an answer is right because of what you know, and thinking an answer is right because it looks or sounds like it should be right.

Summary: To ensure that your selection is appropriately random, make a predetermined selection from among all answer choices you have not eliminated.

Test-Taking Strategies

This section contains a list of test-taking strategies that you may find helpful as you work through the test. By taking what you know and applying logical thought, you can maximize your chances of answering any question correctly!

It is very important to realize that every question is different and every person is different: no single strategy will work on every question, and no single strategy will work for every person. That's why we've included all of them here, so you can try them out and determine which ones work best for different types of questions and which ones work best for you.

Question Strategies

⊘ Read Carefully

Read the question and the answer choices carefully. Don't miss the question because you misread the terms. You have plenty of time to read each question thoroughly and make sure you understand what is being asked. Yet a happy medium must be attained, so don't waste too much time. You must read carefully and efficiently.

⊘ Contextual Clues

Look for contextual clues. If the question includes a word you are not familiar with, look at the immediate context for some indication of what the word might mean. Contextual clues can often give you all the information you need to decipher the meaning of an unfamiliar word. Even if you can't determine the meaning, you may be able to narrow down the possibilities enough to make a solid guess at the answer to the question.

⊘ Prefixes

If you're having trouble with a word in the question or answer choices, try dissecting it. Take advantage of every clue that the word might include. Prefixes can be a huge help. Usually, they allow you to determine a basic meaning. *Pre-* means before, *post-* means after, *pro-* is positive, *de-* is negative. From prefixes, you can get an idea of the general meaning of the word and try to put it into context.

⊘ Hedge Words

Watch out for critical hedge words, such as *likely, may, can, often, almost, mostly, usually, generally, rarely*, and *sometimes*. Question writers insert these hedge phrases to cover every possibility. Often an answer choice will be wrong simply because it leaves no room for exception. Be on guard for answer choices that have definitive words such as *exactly* and *always*.

⊘ Switchback Words

Stay alert for *switchbacks*. These are the words and phrases frequently used to alert you to shifts in thought. The most common switchback words are *but, although*, and *however*. Others include *nevertheless, on the other hand, even though, while, in spite of, despite*, and *regardless of*. Switchback words are important to catch because they can change the direction of the question or an answer choice.

✓ Face Value

When in doubt, use common sense. Accept the situation in the problem at face value. Don't read too much into it. These problems will not require you to make wild assumptions. If you have to go beyond creativity and warp time or space in order to have an answer choice fit the question, then you should move on and consider the other answer choices. These are normal problems rooted in reality. The applicable relationship or explanation may not be readily apparent, but it is there for you to figure out. Use your common sense to interpret anything that isn't clear.

Answer Choice Strategies

✓ Answer Selection

The most thorough way to pick an answer choice is to identify and eliminate wrong answers until only one is left, then confirm it is the correct answer. Sometimes an answer choice may immediately seem right, but be careful. The test writers will usually put more than one reasonable answer choice on each question, so take a second to read all of them and make sure that the other choices are not equally obvious. As long as you have time left, it is better to read every answer choice than to pick the first one that looks right without checking the others.

✓ Answer Choice Families

An answer choice family consists of two (in rare cases, three) answer choices that are very similar in construction and cannot all be true at the same time. If you see two answer choices that are direct opposites or parallels, one of them is usually the correct answer. For instance, if one answer choice says that quantity *x* increases and another either says that quantity *x* decreases (opposite) or says that quantity *y* increases (parallel), then those answer choices would fall into the same family. An answer choice that doesn't match the construction of the answer choice family is more likely to be incorrect. Most questions will not have answer choice families, but when they do appear, you should be prepared to recognize them.

✓ Eliminate Answers

Eliminate answer choices as soon as you realize they are wrong, but make sure you consider all possibilities. If you are eliminating answer choices and realize that the last one you are left with is also wrong, don't panic. Start over and consider each choice again. There may be something you missed the first time that you will realize on the second pass.

✓ Avoid Fact Traps

Don't be distracted by an answer choice that is factually true but doesn't answer the question. You are looking for the choice that answers the question. Stay focused on what the question is asking for so you don't accidentally pick an answer that is true but incorrect. Always go back to the question and make sure the answer choice you've selected actually answers the question and is not merely a true statement.

✓ Extreme Statements

In general, you should avoid answers that put forth extreme actions as standard practice or proclaim controversial ideas as established fact. An answer choice that states the "process should be used in certain situations, if..." is much more likely to be correct than one that states the "process should be discontinued completely." The first is a calm rational statement and doesn't even make a definitive, uncompromising stance, using a hedge word *if* to provide wiggle room, whereas the second choice is far more extreme.

⊘ Benchmark

As you read through the answer choices and you come across one that seems to answer the question well, mentally select that answer choice. This is not your final answer, but it's the one that will help you evaluate the other answer choices. The one that you selected is your benchmark or standard for judging each of the other answer choices. Every other answer choice must be compared to your benchmark. That choice is correct until proven otherwise by another answer choice beating it. If you find a better answer, then that one becomes your new benchmark. Once you've decided that no other choice answers the question as well as your benchmark, you have your final answer.

⊘ Predict the Answer

Before you even start looking at the answer choices, it is often best to try to predict the answer. When you come up with the answer on your own, it is easier to avoid distractions and traps because you will know exactly what to look for. The right answer choice is unlikely to be word-for-word what you came up with, but it should be a close match. Even if you are confident that you have the right answer, you should still take the time to read each option before moving on.

General Strategies

⊘ Tough Questions

If you are stumped on a problem or it appears too hard or too difficult, don't waste time. Move on! Remember though, if you can quickly check for obviously incorrect answer choices, your chances of guessing correctly are greatly improved. Before you completely give up, at least try to knock out a couple of possible answers. Eliminate what you can and then guess at the remaining answer choices before moving on.

⊘ Check Your Work

Since you will probably not know every term listed and the answer to every question, it is important that you get credit for the ones that you do know. Don't miss any questions through careless mistakes. If at all possible, try to take a second to look back over your answer selection and make sure you've selected the correct answer choice and haven't made a costly careless mistake (such as marking an answer choice that you didn't mean to mark). This quick double check should more than pay for itself in caught mistakes for the time it costs.

⊘ Pace Yourself

It's easy to be overwhelmed when you're looking at a page full of questions; your mind is confused and full of random thoughts, and the clock is ticking down faster than you would like. Calm down and maintain the pace that you have set for yourself. Especially as you get down to the last few minutes of the test, don't let the small numbers on the clock make you panic. As long as you are on track by monitoring your pace, you are guaranteed to have time for each question.

⊘ Don't Rush

It is very easy to make errors when you are in a hurry. Maintaining a fast pace in answering questions is pointless if it makes you miss questions that you would have gotten right otherwise. Test writers like to include distracting information and wrong answers that seem right. Taking a little extra time to avoid careless mistakes can make all the difference in your test score. Find a pace that allows you to be confident in the answers that you select.

✓ KEEP MOVING

Panicking will not help you pass the test, so do your best to stay calm and keep moving. Taking deep breaths and going through the answer elimination steps you practiced can help to break through a stress barrier and keep your pace.

Final Notes

The combination of a solid foundation of content knowledge and the confidence that comes from practicing your plan for applying that knowledge is the key to maximizing your performance on test day. As your foundation of content knowledge is built up and strengthened, you'll find that the strategies included in this chapter become more and more effective in helping you quickly sift through the distractions and traps of the test to isolate the correct answer.

Now that you're preparing to move forward into the test content chapters of this book, be sure to keep your goal in mind. As you read, think about how you will be able to apply this information on the test. If you've already seen sample questions for the test and you have an idea of the question format and style, try to come up with questions of your own that you can answer based on what you're reading. This will give you valuable practice applying your knowledge in the same ways you can expect to on test day.

Good luck and good studying!

Basic Economic Concepts

Capital

Capital is a comprehensive term for all or any methods by which products are made by labor. This includes a wide variety of tools or elements. **Physical capital** may include all categories of real objects such as equipment, plants, land, and machinery that contribute to the process of production. **Intellectual capital** is the necessary ingredient that transforms the production process by human interaction. Included in intellectual capital is the utilization of information, management skills, and technological advances, as well as the application of ideas and theories which are catalysts in the economic system.

Although capital is generally regarded as an essential ingredient of benign economic activity, it can also be used to foster the **defense** of a state or prepare a country for an aggressive war. Large portions of Germany's capital were used by the Nazis in their attempt to dominate Europe. Capital is commonly used to further a state's **geopolitical aims** through peaceful or belligerent goals. The utilization of capital is a prime indicator of any country's goals and ambitions.

Historically, capital was considered to be physical equipment, machinery, plants, and other major investments used in manufacturing. The more modern concept of capital broadens the definition to include a wide range of **assets** that are utilized in the production process.

Financial capitalrepresents the operating funds and monetary investment in a business or plant. Financial capital is often obtained by corporations through the issue of stock in exchange for funds. Natural resources such as oceans, forests, mountains, and rivers provide **natural capital** which may or may not be publicly owned. Capital that is used to provide support systems for fundamental production processes and operating ability is sometimes termed **infrastructural capital**. Much of this type of capital is represented in plants and equipment. The abilities and acumen gained from education and experience are sometimes referred to as **human capital**. This incorporates the many types of growth and development from what we call human resources.

Factors of Production

Resources that are used in the production and manufacture of goods and services are called **factors of production**. They include land and natural products derived from land, including dirt, gems, minerals, and fodder. The cost of using land is usually rent in one form or another. Labor is another factor of production, and this is a blanket term for all individuals involved in the manufacturing, marketing, and transfer of goods and services. The payment for labor is designated as wages. Capital is the third essential factor of production. These definitions of the factors of production are from classical economics and political economy, and they remain accurate today, although the idea of capital has been expanded to include human expertise and technology.

Foundation of Economics as a Science

The study of economics includes **microeconomics**, which is concerned with smaller units, such as individuals and firms, and **macroeconomics**, which looks at the economy as a composite, taking a more global view. In general, economics deals with topics such as scarcity, supply, demand, and choices made by various parts of the economy and the total economy. There are a variety of economic topics that overlap both microeconomics and macroeconomics. These hybrid areas may be covered separately or as a part of the micro/macroeconomic spectrum. "Mainstream" economics is a blend of macroeconomics and economic theory developed in the last 50 years. This includes a number of schools of economic thought, each with its own assumptions, conclusions, and methodology. Economics centers on the idea of scarce resources and how to best utilize these resources to meet the needs of individuals and the economic system as a whole.

Mechanism Where the Study of Economics Occurs

The exchange of services and goods in an organized marketplace, where sellers and buyers vie to optimize their results by trading, is the **mechanism where the study of economics occurs**. Factors of production, the directed use of labor and capital, and the achievement of profit are the driving forces of an economic system. The clearest representation of these elements occurs in a **free market economy**, of which capitalism is the prime example. These factors are also in play in **state-controlled systems**, which include communism and socialism. Many contend that in all economic systems, the driving force is self-interest, or the "Invisible Hand" that Adam Smith defined in his Wealth of Nations. Economics may be studied in a wide spectrum of political, social, and financial systems. Commonalities and contrasts may be used as a method of comparing economic theory in a variety of settings. Many of the crucial components of economics are active in any organized society, regardless of its philosophy.

Beginnings of Economics as a Science

Political economy was defined as the economics of **competing states**, and was the term used by early economic thinkers. Neoclassical economists discarded this term in the late 1800s in favor of simply *economics*. The origin of the term *economics* is from the Greek word *oikonomikos*, meaning settlement laws. Economics was a recognized field in early Greek, Arab, and Roman eras. This is known as the **premodern period**. The mercantile and physiocrat systems are termed **early modern**, and what we now call economics is named **modern economics** in the history of economic thought. The pioneers of modern economic thought include such giants as Karl Marx, David Ricardo, John Stuart Mill, and of course, Adam Smith. Economic references and problems are discussed in early texts such as the Old and New Testaments. Economic thought has often played an important part in political systems such as Communism and Socialism and has played a major role in all societies.

Foundation of Modern Economics

Modern economics is based on one basic premise: that **resources** are scarce and limited, and that **choices** must be made in the acquisition and use of them. All other questions and alternatives flow from this assumption. Economic choices involve sacrificing something in order to obtain another thing. This sacrifice is called the "**opportunity cost**" of the choice. You may choose to spend your last dollar on a candy bar rather than a writing tablet, thus the opportunity cost of the candy bar is the tablet. There are seemingly endless choices in a consumer society, all of which involve choices and opportunity costs. The choices and opportunity costs are expressed in price relationships in modern economics. Each individual makes many economic decisions (choices) each day, and the aggregate reflects the economic activity of a society. Choices are driven by the **utility**, or want-satisfying abilities of the goods and services. Choices are ranked on the ability of the good or service to fill a perceived need of the individual. This utility function is active in most, but not all, economic choices.

Scarcity and Choice

Economics could rightfully be called the study of **scarcity**. Limited resources are available to satisfy the wants and needs of both individuals and states. Economics involves the **choices** made by an economy to satisfy these wants and needs. Every economy must choose what goods and services to produce, how to produce them, and for whom they are intended. Limitations of the factors of production—land, labor, and capital—sometimes make these choices difficult. When an economic choice is made, there is an "**opportunity cost**" implicit in the choice. The opportunity cost is what is given up by making a choice. If a country chooses to manufacture automobiles, it may not have the industrial capacity to produce tanks or aircraft. Thus, the economic choice to make automobiles involves the opportunity cost of not making tanks or aircraft. Individuals and countries continually make economic choices and sacrifice opportunist costs in the process. An individual may choose to attend a film rather than go out to dinner. Choices are driven by what people and countries feel is in their best interest.

Specialization and Division of Labor

Labor, a major factor of production, must be used in the most efficient manner to optimize the economic system. The concept of **specialization** requires that labor (and other factors of production) be used on work on which they are most efficient in order to produce goods in the most cost-effective manner. This means allocating specialized operations to various members of the workforce so each can concentrate on what he or she does best. The result should be an increase in productivity with a corresponding increased profitability of the firm. When this concept is extrapolated throughout an economy, it provides a country with a competitive advantage, that is to say, a nation, company, or individual will be producing most efficiently, giving a boost to productivity. Such an economy will tend to have an edge in international trade, and function more efficiently in the domestic economy.

Market Economy

A market economy is an economic system in which the **individuals** own and operate all factors related to production. It relies on **entrepreneurship** to spur markets for operation. The goal of individuals in a market economy is to obtain a profit from their chosen area of business. It is often associated with capitalism and private ownership of capital. Market economies are successful in part due to increased individual freedom for their members. When people have the freedom to make their own decisions, the economy is more likely to function efficiently. This is because changes in the markets will be noticed and responded to quickly and appropriately. There is more flexibility for economic action in a market economy system. Through private ownership and individual freedom, market economies are the most successful systems for the operations of free markets in the world. The largest market economies today are the United States, China, and Japan.

Review Video: Basics of Market Economy
Visit mometrix.com/academy and enter code: 791556

Economics in the Premodern Age

Ibn Khaldun of Tunis, writing in the 12th century, discussed political and economic theory. A favorite subject of his was population density and its effect on economic cycles. This is one of the earliest records of economic theory. **Scholasticism**, a theological school of philosophy in the Middle Ages, incorporated a debate over a number of basic economic issues, including how a fair price of something could be determined. In the wars between the Church and her reformers during the **Reformation**, the concept of free trade arose and was considered in both theological and political contexts. The church and nobility saw economic activity as a way to raise revenues, and imposed taxes on almost all transactions. These taxes were used to finance wars and enrich the ruling classes, almost never benefiting those being taxed. **Feudalism** imposed its own system of economics, determining how most economic affairs would be conducted and taxed. Needless to say, the serfs rarely saw any good from these measures.

Early Stirrings of Economic Thought

The **Mercantilists**, a group of European importers and exporters, strove to profit from exploring new markets, trading goods at a profitable rate, and growing their markets. Mercantilists were the dominant economic force in the new nation-states of Europe. Their activities were instrumental in leading to the discovery and settlement of the New World. The **Physiocrats**, a school of eco-philosophy active in France during the Enlightenment, were led by writers such as Anne Turgot and Francois Quesnay. Arguably, this was the first school or movement that viewed economics as a field in its own right. Many believe that modern economics was founded by the Physiocrats. Later thinkers and writers such as Adam Smith and David Ricardo built their theories on the foundation laid by the Physiocrats. As a group, the Physiocrats were short-lived, but their impact was significant in the development of economic thought.

TIMELINE OF ECONOMIC SCHOOLS OF THOUGHT THROUGH THE CENTURIES

Schools of economic thought may be loosely categorized as follows:

- **16th-18th Century** - Dominated by the European nation-states who pioneered Mercantilism in an effort to enrich themselves through trade and exploration of new markets. The Physiocrats were an important 18th-century economic school that originated in France.
- **18th-19th Century** - Great economic thinkers and philosophers such as Adam Smith, John Stuart Mill, Thomas Malthus, and David Ricardo wrote important works that provided the foundation for Classical economics. This period also saw the rise of the "Utopian Socialists," who formulated economic ideas to cure the ills of society. Marxism is also included in this period, although it mixes political, social, and economic theory in a hybrid philosophy.
- **Late 19th Century** - Alfred Marshall is felt to be the father of Neoclassical economics. Marshall authored the concept of "marginal theory of value," which is the cornerstone of neoclassical economics.
- **20th Century** - Carl Menger wrote the seminal work on economics for what was to be called the Austrian school. The American Institutionalist school and German school of economics appeared during this period.

PRINCIPLE OF COMPARATIVE ADVANTAGE

Why would two countries continue to trade if one can produce goods and services cheaper than another? The answer is a **comparative advantage**, which depends upon the ratio between the costs of producing different products. This concept was introduced by **David Ricardo** in his seminal work on political economy and trade. Essentially, the principle states that each nation should specialize in producing the commodity with the lower opportunity cost. This would give the country a comparative advantage in exporting that product. It should trade with another country for a product for which it has a comparative disadvantage. Thus, each country will benefit from buying goods abroad that are more costly to produce at home. **Competitive advantage** is the principle that makes international commerce work effectively. If a country does not have a competitive advantage in a product, there must be other reasons for that country to trade.

COMMAND ECONOMY

A command economy is one in which the government controls basic economic activities. Such an economy is directed by decisions of one group (the ruling class) for all members of the society. Such a system, typical in dictatorships, suffers because of the lack of private interest in economic success. Command economies are slower to respond to changing economic fluctuations, as they are controlled by cumbersome organizations and not responsive to the “invisible hand” of self-interest. Socialism and communism are examples of command economies today.

Marginalism

Marginalism concerns itself with the economic worth of the last (or next) product or service provided. The cost of making the last product, the cost of hiring the last employee, and the cost of selling the last product, determine the **marginal cost** of that next good. Presumably, a company will continue to produce goods and services until it becomes unprofitable. Production will cease when the marginal return of a product does not yield a profit. From the consumer's viewpoint, the **marginal utility** of the purchase is the crucial factor. How much satisfaction does an individual get from each purchase? When this marginal utility decreases too much, the buyer will not buy the next unit. The idea of diminishing returns often determines how many units of a good or service a buyer will purchase. For example, after eating a piece of pie, the want-satisfying power of the next piece of pie is decreased. When this marginal utility reaches a certain point, the consumer will stop buying.

Opportunity Cost

The opportunity cost of an economic decision is the loss of potential gain from other opportunities when one opportunity is taken. For example, a person may have enough money for a vacation in Europe or a new car but not both. The **opportunity cost** of buying the car will be the trip to Europe. These decisions are made usually on the **utility** of each choice. In other words, determining which choice would provide the most pleasure to the consumer. In a complex economy, there are many competing factors that provide utility. An individual, firm, or government will always choose what they perceive to be the best choice given limited resources. These choices are usually not clear-cut, and many factors go into some economic decisions. This is more common when companies or governments have to choose between a number of needed and attractive choices. Different parts of society will have different ideas about the best way to use their resources.

Criticisms of Marginality

Marginal utility is founded on **subjectivity**, rather than **objectivity**. Marginal utility places its focus on buying and selling transactions between individual units in the economy, to the exclusion of the activity of the economy as a whole. The marketplace is the Holy Grail for the proponents of marginal utility, who see the markets as the foundation of economic activity. The production function is ignored; this is a crucial error, as costs of production are a major determinant of prices, and, therefore, all microeconomic activity. Critics of marginal utility say it is impossible to understand **consumer utility**, which is determined in part by prices. The prices themselves are based on consumer preferences, making an accurate analysis difficult if not impossible. Another area of criticism for the concept of marginal utility is that it often attempts to correlate utility with price. This correlation does not hold true where a product may be useful and necessary to an individual but cost nothing. An example of this would be water.

Production in Depth

The production function in microeconomics refers to the total process of **producing or assembling** goods and services that are to be traded in a marketplace. Production decisions are some of the most vital in microeconomics. A firm or individual must decide what to make and how many units to provide. This will often depend on the method of production and the unit price of making each product. An evaluation of the necessary resources to be utilized is another important production decision. In tandem with sophisticated market research, optimum decisions can be made about producing goods and services. Production is a process, and, as such, it occurs through time and space. Because it is a flow concept, an important statistic is the amount of production for a specific period of time. Other factors of concern are the amount and physical dimensions of the finished process. This will be important in storing and shipping the finished goods.

Efficiency and X-Efficiency

The measurement of the productivity of a production process is vital. Productivity may be said to be **efficient** when the optimum number of finished products is produced with a minimum of raw materials, assuming quality control is maintained. If a production operation is less productive than anticipated, due to internal or external forces, it is said to be **X-efficient**. Such X-efficient production operations are often due to a number of factors beyond the control of the producer. Examples would be shortages of raw materials, increased and unexpected competition, or problems in the supply of necessary labor. The productivity of a production function is simply based on how many units of a finished product can be made from a minimum amount of inputs. The more efficient processes give firms an important competitive position and greater flexibility in pricing and marketing. Decisions made about production will often determine the success or failure of the product line for a firm.

Factors of Production

Factors of production are the sum total of the resources needed to produce finished goods. The major **factors** identified by economists include the use of land (for factories and agricultural products), labor (the human workforce), natural resources (raw materials used in manufacturing), and capital goods (previously manufactured equipment used in production). Human inputs such as management and human relations could be added to the mix. Contemporary economists often include technological expertise in the factors of production. Factors of production may be **fixed** (one which cannot be changed) or **variable** (one which can be adjusted by management easily). Examples of fixed factors would be physical plants, heavy machinery, and key managerial personnel. A variable factor of production is one whose usage rate can be changed easily. In the "long run" all of these factors of production can be adjusted by management. The "short run," however, is defined as a period in which at least one of the factors of production is fixed.

Diminishing Marginal Returns Analysis

As additional raw materials and resources are added to production factors, a point occurs where the production function becomes less efficient. In other words, additional resources are yielding less-profitable final products. This point is called the **point of diminishing returns** and is measured as a position on the marginal physical production curve. Continuing production will eventually result in producing products that lose money. Thus, it would be preferable to stop production. **Diminishing marginal returns** will vary from industry to industry, depending on the necessary factors of production needed to produce goods and services. The combination of land, labor, and capital needed for production is different for each product, so the point of diminishing marginal return will also differ. Demand, supply, and price changes in the factors of production will all impact this analysis.

Production Functions

Production functions, an important area of analysis in microeconomics, concerns itself with the ratio of raw materials or resources needed to produce a certain amount of goods and services. This relationship may be depicted as a mathematical one or illustrated with a graph. The goal of analyzing the production functions is to **optimize** the number of finished goods that can be obtained from the minimum of inputs. Many factors enter into such an analysis, including supply and demand of the factors of production, state-of-the-art technology, and managerial skill. Every production function will be different because of the mix of factors for producing different goods at various times. If a producer knows the exact quantity of finished goods he or she must manufacture, the **production function** would be the **minimum necessary resources** needed to achieve that production number. Current technology will affect this combination of resources. In this type of analysis, costs and prices are not considered.

Criticism

Controversy has surrounded the validity of production function analysis. Most of the **criticism** is concerned with how certain factors of production were measured and how proportions of the factors were mixed. Some economists feel it is not possible to post a necessary amount of capital without a complete understanding of both interest rates and the cost of labor. The production function analysis must include specific prices for all factors of production, but the analysis itself depends on knowing these variables. This is the "which came first, the chicken or the egg" problem. Exact variables cannot be known until the production function analysis is complete, but the analysis is the method of determining the variables. Special mathematical constructs and assumptions must be built in these models of production functioned to have a useful function.

Production Possibility Curve

When any product is made, there is an opportunity cost of forgoing using the resources to make a different product. If two or more items are being produced at the same time, there will be **opportunity costs** involved in decisions regarding the relative amount of each product to produce. This analysis is called the **production possibility curve**. The production possibility curve is a valuable tool for manufacturers because it explores production alternatives and their economic result. Points of **maximum productivity** may be plotted using this graphical tool, which will also illuminate when production becomes **inefficient**. Companies can then choose optimum mixes of products as well as determine when a finished good is not economically feasible to manufacture. The analysis should yield the necessary information for a firm to adjust their product mix and quantities of goods produced to the most profitable level.

Cost-Benefit Analysis

The determination of the best possible economic action in a situation is often formally or intuitively a result of a **cost-benefit computation**. An individual must ask what the total costs will be in any decision in relation to the total benefits, which may be reasonably predicted. Analyzing several alternatives using this approach will yield the best decision given the information available. In business decisions, this usually means determining what amount of resources must be used to gain a specified return or profit. Such cost-benefit calculations are not limited to money. Subjective factors must be considered and sometimes an arbitrary monetary value placed on them. Economic decisions, particularly on the part of governments, must weigh economic, quality-of-life, political, and social elements into this analysis. For example, a government decision to drill for oil in a natural habitat will include economic considerations, as well as the impact of the decision on the well-being of the society as a whole. Since almost all economic actions occur over time, future costs and profits must be considered from a **present-value perspective**.

Consumer Preference

Microeconomics is concerned with individual decisions that ultimately affect the entire economy. Consumer behavior is an important aspect of microeconomics. **Consumer preferences** are difficult to assess, because of the seemingly endless choices, conscious and unconscious, that motivate consumer behavior. Economic models have been constructed to better understand consumer activities. These are sometimes called **preference relations** (charting consumers' preferences). These models of consumer preferences have many flaws, but they can attempt to predict the behavior of buyers under various sets of conditions. A major flaw may be termed the completeness of understanding consumer behavior. Although a preference model may be able to show in theory how consumers will behave under a set of economic conditions, it is impossible to measure all the factors that enter into choices made by buyers. These choices are subject to rapid change due to external economic changes.

Determining Ideal Firm Size

Determining the optimum size of a company provides a challenge for managers. Because businesses are measured, in large part, by their profitability, the size of a firm should ideally be that which provides the **greatest profit**. This size will vary greatly between various companies, industries, and geographical locations. The ideal size of a firm is a fluid variable, changing with economic and competitive fluctuations. Economies and diseconomies of scale, scope, and agglomeration will all contribute to the determination of an **ideal business size**. Particular industries tend to affect the size of firms. For example, manufacturers of heavy equipment, with large labor and capital demands, tend to be larger than candy manufacturers, whose needs differ dramatically. Managers must constantly be attentive to their business' competitive position, costs, market share, and growth potential to adequately predict the ideal size of their companies. A fluid business environment makes these decisions difficult but crucial.

History of Money

Money has been defined as any store of value which has **intrinsic value** or is a **representation** of a store of value (banknotes). Money is the lifeblood of **market transactions**, serving as a measure of value, a medium of exchange, and a convention of accounting. As a means to exchange value for goods and services, money has no peer. But for this to be the case, money must have a guaranteed and obvious value of its own. Historically, commodities including crops and livestock were the first forms of money. When money became accepted as a representation of commodities, the market system was revolutionized. It made trading easy, and quickly became an accepted medium of exchange. In earlier times, money represented the commodities of precious metals, notably gold and silver. In modern economies, money depends on the guarantee of the government to honor its value. These guarantees permit international trade without risk about the value of the money involved.

Forms of Money

The first items considered as "money" were commodities that were traded under a **barter system**. The next advance in the form of money was the minting of **coins** of precious metals, usually silver and gold. This form of money had intrinsic value but was a very limited resource. It could be transported fairly easily in moderate amounts and was difficult to forge. The next leap in the form of money was the advent of **paper notes**, issued and guaranteed by governments. In modern economies, money has taken on a variety of new forms, some a result of increasing technological advances. Modern economies feature paper notes backed by the central bank and government that issues them. Coins with a small percentage of silver or gold are also assets honored by central banks. The intrinsic value of precious metals in most coins is negligible. By far the most revolutionary change in the form of money has occurred in the last 100 years. Demand deposits, credit cards, commercial paper, certificates of deposit, mortgages, and public and private promissory notes are all a form of money today.

John Maynard Keynes

Perhaps the most influential economist of the last 100 years was **John Maynard Keynes**. Born in 1883, Keynes lived his life and developed his theories in England during the first quarter of the 20th century. Although a great proponent of government intervention in managing the economy, Keynes was strongly opposed to socialism, which he felt would weaken a free economy. Keynes's major concerns were the management and control of business cycles, eliminating both depressions and inflation, which he saw as destabilizing economic systems. His major thesis was that **aggregate**

demand was the most important indicator of economic cycles, particularly the extremes of depression and runaway inflation.

Keynes summarized his theories in *The General Theory of Employment, Interest, and Money*, which he wrote in the early 1930s. Keynes's ideas gained international acclaim and were the basis for the active government role in combating the depression in the 1930s. His ideas appeal to those who believe the responsibility of the government is to act strongly to encourage economic growth.

Robert Lucas Jr.

Robert Lucas Jr. is regarded as one of the most important contemporary economists. A professor of Economics at the University of Chicago, Lucas was instrumental in applying microeconomic analytical methods to study the economy as a whole. His work on the theory of "**Rational Expectations**" was groundbreaking and added greatly to his reputation as a leading economist. He was awarded the Nobel Prize for this work in 1995. The "**Lucas Technique**" investigates the dynamic relationships in an economy. It analyzes the cause-and-effect determination of such economic indicators as employment, inflation, government policies in economics, and the role of monetary policy in affecting economic activity. Creator of the famous "**Lucas islands**" model of monetary influence among consumers, he has earned a place of international respect from economists all over the world. Lucas remains an active researcher and economic theorist today.

Robert Mundell

Robert Mundell is another leading contemporary macroeconomist. A professor at Columbia University, Mundell is a leading figure in the development of **supply-side economics**. He was awarded the Nobel Prize in Economics in 1999 for his overall contributions to economic theory. Mundell pioneered theory on **optimal currency areas**, which reflected his interest in the role of currencies in the economic fluctuations of countries. This work established him as an expert on money and currency, and Mundell was active in the development of the **euro** for the European Union. His work in advocating supply-side economics is well known, and he is known as a leading expert on the gold standard and its historical implications. Mundell was hailed as a prophet when he accurately predicted the rampant inflation of the 1970s. He has developed several important economic models, including the **Mundell-Fleming model** and the **Mundell-Tobin effect**.

Finn Erling Kydland

A Norwegian economist who won the Nobel Prize in Economics in 2004 for his research and models of macroeconomic systems, **Kydland** currently holds a teaching position at the University of California. Kydland has immersed himself in the study of the impact of government economic policy over a period of years. His work on the understanding of the **fluctuations of business cycles** is classic, and he is regarded as a pioneer in applying **mathematical models** to the analysis of economic activity. A leading thinker in political economy and macroeconomics, Kydland has done primary and secondary research on the effects of fiscal and monetary policy on business cycles. Labor economics is another specialty of his, and he is regarded as one of the most important of the labor economists. The relationships between the availability, cost, and demand for labor on economic cycles are of paramount interest to Kydland.

Edward Prescott

A major macroeconomist of the day is **Edward Prescott**. A close collaborator of Finn Kydland, with whom he shared the Nobel Prize in economics in 2004, Prescott currently serves as an economist for the Federal Reserve System. He has concentrated his economic interests in the areas of **general equilibrium** and **fluctuations of economic activity**. His particular field of interest is the role of central banks in applying monetary policy to affect business cycles. He addresses the question of whether central banks should be given wide-ranging power to increase or decrease the money supply in an attempt to avoid economic extremes. Prescott developed the **Hodrick-Prescott model of strategies** to even the ups and downs of business cycles. This was widely hailed by economists as a major breakthrough in the management of economic fluctuations in an economy. Prescott currently engages in monetary and fiscal research, as well as holding several teaching positions in economics.

Developmental Economics

Developing countries have unique economic problems that more sophisticated economies do not. Particularly important is the area of long-term economic growth in developing economies. This field is called **developmental economics**. It also includes the microeconomic analyses of individuals and firms in such fledgling economies. It is a highly analytical field that uses **econometrics** (mathematical applications to economics) to predict economic patterns. Usually, both mathematical and qualitative tools are used to measure and predict economic activity in developing countries. Included in the field are the problems of long-term debt and the action of international economic agencies such as the International Monetary Fund. The problem of encouraging and sustaining economic growth in such countries is a primary objective of economists. The field includes not only economic issues and tools but also social and political methods to influence the whole society.

Political Economy

Political economics is an umbrella term that includes a wide variety of economic approaches to study and predict behavior. It often uses techniques and tools from other social sciences in its applications. **Political economy** is a maverick in economic theory, as it often contravenes accepted economic doctrine. Interdisciplinary by definition, political economy studies the interactions of social and political factors on economic issues that affect markets. The term was originally used in political science to compare and contrast relationships of geopolitics between countries. A number of political-social-economic schools have made political economy their main interest. The historical long-term implications of political economy are of great interest to economic historians.

Transport, Exchange, Infrastructure, and Consumption

Transportation is the network that allows the economy to function. Capital and labor must be moved to land in order to facilitate production. Finished goods must be moved through channels of distribution to be available to consumers. **Transport** is necessary for the movement of products, people, and capital. **Economic exchange** is the basic activity of economics. The circular cycle of exchange from consumer to suppliers and back are the transactions that move an economy. The field of exchange is the marketplace, and money is the medium through which these transactions move. Building an **infrastructure** for market transactions is necessary to allow an orderly and dependable mechanism for economic exchange. **Consumption** of goods, services, and ancillary products is the final activity for satisfying the needs and wants of society. Consumption also may include the less tangible qualities of health, leisure activity, goodwill, and freedom of choice.

Disposal

All excess products of consumption or production must be eliminated as **waste**. The failure to dispose of these waste products will result in an impaired economy and a degradation of the quality of life. Waste removal requires a large physical capacity and the employment of significant capital resources. The increasing urbanization of the world makes **waste disposal** an important priority. Systems of waste removal include garbage and sewage operations as well as preventative measures of recycling and legislation to protect the environment. Governments must take responsibility for waste removal because of the scope of the problem. The ecological movement and "green" economics of the past 30 years have raised questions on the economics of waste and the quality of life. This has generated increased concern about such issues as destruction of natural habitats, global warming, air and water pollution, and the importance of sustaining our natural resources.

"The Market"

The central arena of political economy is the **marketplace** where economic activity occurs. It is also the intersecting point of the sometimes competing economic interests and forces at play. Common causes may be found by unlikely allies, and groups may be pitted against each other for economic advantage. In a **capitalistic economic system**, the major task of the state is the creation and preservation of capital and the economic choices involved in its allocation. **Socialism** maintains that decisions and implementation of production should be determined by the power of the state, ostensibly to create the greatest good for the most people. This philosophy brings socialism into conflict with capitalism, which requires that fundamental economic power should be in private hands. **Communism** seeks control over all factors of production as well as political and social dominance over its society.

"Adaptive Expectations"

When individuals base their expectations on past economic events and history, it is called "**adaptive expectations**." An example would be if the stock market has been strong for a period of time, the public will have positive expectations for future advances. Individuals will base their future economic decisions on the cumulative experience of recent economic activity. These decisions will become self-fulfilling if consumers are pessimistic about the future of the economy. An example of adaptive expectations is the general attitude regarding inflation. In the United States, as well as most of the free world, inflation has become a fact of economic life. The expectation of rising prices, increasing wages, and general cost-of-living increases has bred a culture of inflationary expectation that rarely fails to materialize. Sometimes, general pessimism about the economy serves as a deterrent to economic expansion. This is another example of adaptive expectations at work.

Gresham's Law

When two or more types of money are commonly used in an economy, and each is assigned the same value by the country, problems may arise. **Thomas Gresham**, a 15th-century English financial genius, stated that money that has a market value lower than its buying power will drive out a form of money that has **stronger consumption value**. People will tend to keep this "good money" as a store of value and spend the "bad money" to exchange for goods and services. This situation can only happen if two different forms of money are in circulation and the state decrees them to have equal value, when in fact they do not. Given a choice of exchanging good or bad money for goods and services people will always spend the bad money and retain the good money. Thus, as **Gresham's law** states, bad money will drive good money out of circulation. This becomes a serious economic problem if people are hoarding good money as a store of value and using bad money in the marketplace. Soon, all the good money will disappear as people hoard it.

Consumption

When a resource is used and eliminated, it has been **consumed**. Consumption is an important feature of economics, usually meaning personal consumption of goods and services. Consumption has its own determinants, including economic expectations, level of disposable income, and the propensity to consume. Ultimately consumption is a component of aggregate demand in economic theory. Economics makes a clear distinction between **production**, the supplying of goods and services, and the **consumption** of these goods and services. Economic research into consumption raises questions regarding the motivation and reasons for various levels of consumption. The relatively recent importance of our consumer society has placed this element of economic theory under the microscope of analysis. Consumption in all its forms has developed a significant impact on the lives of everyone in a modern economy.

Labor Economics

As in all the factors of production, **labor** has a separate market based on supply and demand. The interaction between employers and workers is the frame of reference of **labor economics**. The result of these interactions affect labor economics and determine income, employment, and wage levels. Labor economics is a vital field since most countries include maximized employment as an economic priority. When labor economics is studied through the individuals and their role in labor markets, microeconomic methods are used. The larger interactions between labor markets and the demand for goods and services, production, consumption, and investment fall under macroeconomic analysis. Both are necessary and useful methods for evaluating the role that labor plays in economic activity. Most of us are more aware of the macroeconomics of labor, which tends to be in the news more often as trends of unemployment and productivity.

Commodity Markets

Commodities are raw or unfinished components of finished goods yet to be produced. Agricultural products such as soybeans, cotton, and wheat are commodities. Separate markets exist for almost all commodities. Currencies of various countries are also traded as commodities in their own markets. Futures markets exist on many heavily traded commodities, where speculation fuels trading for future delivery of products paid for now. Commodities were one of the first classes of goods traded between countries. Modern **commodity markets** have been safeguarded by a bevy of rules and regulations ensuring prompt and accurate payment between countries. International agencies, such as the Bank for International Settlements, regulate transaction settlements, insure currencies, set reserve requirements, and generally reduce risks in trade inherent between countries.

Store of Value

Any form of money or capital including commodities may be seen as a **store of value** if it meets certain standards. Any store of value must be readily stored, retrieved, and saved. The store of value must retain its value over time, both as intrinsic wealth and the ability to use it to settle debts. Many assets have been used as a store of value over the centuries. Precious metals, primarily gold and silver, have been historical favorites. The most stable currencies extant at a historical point also may serve as a store of value. When the British Empire was powerful, the pound sterling was often used as the store of value. Real estate has always been known as a reliable store of value, and art, antiques, and rare collections have also served this purpose. Many of these are not practical for daily trading, which includes immediate settling of accounts. The common feature is that they all have **intrinsic value** and rarely lose it. There is always a more or less stable demand for these items.

High Technology Economics

Many economists and investors feel that the sector of the economy using cutting-edge **high technological methods** is the most promising for economic growth. This conclusion has promoted increasing and sometimes speculative investment in high-tech fields. But as the world learned from the anticipated boom in information technology, reality does not always meet expectations. The so-called "dot-com" boom in the last 20 years saw the making of great fortunes but also the loss of investments when companies failed to meet their expected growth. High technology economics still offers uncommon rewards for the astute investor, but must also be regarded as very high risk for investors. Areas usually associated with high technology advances include nanotechnology, information technology, and biotechnology, among many others. High technology industries flourish across the world, making constant progress in developing new techniques and applications for multiple growth industries.

The Invisible Hand

One of the fundamental concepts of classical economics is the "**invisible guiding hand of self-interest**" that posits each individual will make economic decisions based on his or her best interests. Developed by **Adam Smith**, the father of capitalism and leading classical economist, the theory states that individuals acting in their own self-interest will also promote the general welfare of all members of the society. Smith felt this was a social mechanism that tended to benefit all. Smith's argument was based on his belief that in a free market economy, people tend to produce goods in demand by consumers. He did not necessarily feel that all self-interested action by itself benefited all of society. Smith's original observations and conclusions are a foundation of classical economics and have been incorporated in one form or another in many schools of economics. Much of **macroeconomic theory** uses the invisible hand concept in postulating economic behavior.

Cost-Of-Production Theory of Value

The concept that the value of an object represents the sum total of all the resources that were involved in producing it is called the **cost-of-production theory of value**. This cost would include any and all of the factors of production utilized in producing the good. Classical economists support the **labor theory-of-value** ideas of Adam Smith, David Ricardo, and Karl Marx. Marx's theory is flawed by his inclusion of the surplus component of value unrelated to the production process. Most contemporary economists reject the cost-of-production theory of value in favor of the marginal theory of value, which contends that an economic value is determined by the marginal utility derived by the consumer in using the product. Some economists distinguish between sectors with **cost-determined** prices and values and **demand-determined** value, which is set by the level of aggregate demand.

Laissez-Faire

The term *laissez-faire* is derived from the French imperative *lassier faire*, meaning to "let do," indicating a hands-off approach. Historically, the term was used by the physiocrats who demanded less governmental influence on international trade. It has become a catch-all phrase for allowing the market the freedom inherent in transactions, without outside influences. Classical economics found a supporter for ***laissez-faire*** in Adam Smith, although he had reservations about some aspects of the policy. A broader definition of *laissez-faire* reflects a style of leadership that allows maximum freedom of individuals to act on their own initiative rather than following orders routinely. It empowers subordinates to make independent decisions and take action on their own. Critics of *laissez-faire* economics point out the failures of lack of any control on economic affairs. The 1920s are sometimes cited as a period in which a lack of government safeguards plunged the country into the Great Depression.

Information Economics

The sub-branch of economics which deals with the use of information in making economic policy and decisions is called **information economics**. Information has unique qualities, being wildly inaccurate at times, easily accessible, and difficult to fully believe. A prime element in economic decisions, information makes accurate and valid choices difficult at times. Information economics studies the mechanisms of economic technology, the value of economic information and its applications, and the asymmetries of information in economics. The market for information is unique. Information is presumably for sale to anyone who will buy it, and it can be sold multiple times. Information has virtually no marginal cost to the buyer. It is easy to duplicate and may be resold many times over. Sometimes information is sold as a bundle. Various sources and pieces of information are combined and sold with or without commentary or suggestions.

REAGANOMICS

The term *Reaganomics* is an umbrella description of the economic policy of the Reagan administration from 1980-1988. These policies faced very high inflation rates and increasing unemployment, a combination called **stagflation**. These dual problems were addressed by applying the principles of **supply-side economics**, combining tax reductions with decreased government spending. Liberal economists and politicians bemoaned the approach as helping the wealthy at the expense of middle- and lower-income individuals. Supply-side economics attempts to encourage investment and expansion through tax cuts and austerity programs rather than stimulating demand. This is the idea of the "trickle-down" approach of economic well-being, beginning at the top. The twin problems of inflation and unemployment were largely solved during the Reagan years, but there is hot debate whether this was caused by economic policy or simply a turn in the business cycle.

THOMAS MALTHUS AND "DISMAL SCIENCE"

Thomas Malthus, the 18th-century economist who named economics the "**dismal science**," felt that population would grow at a rate that would cause people to starve, and the level of population would reach a subsistence level. Malthus's theories have been proved wrong in a large part of the developed world, but his predictions are accurate for many poor third-world countries who suffer periodic **famines**. Industrialized countries have developed technologies to produce food to keep abreast of population growth, which has been slowed by birth control methods. Developing countries with unchecked population explosions and inferior technology often cannot produce enough food to feed themselves. These countries must rely on international aid and relief agencies to provide the essentials of life. Much of the development of third-world nations is geared to increasing food production and introducing methods to slow the population growth. These actions have had mixed success to date.

SIGNIFICANT LITERATURE IN ECONOMICS

THE WEALTH OF NATIONS - ADAM SMITH

The book is usually considered to be the beginning of **modern economics**. It begins with a discussion of the Industrial Revolution. Later, it critiques mercantilism and a synthesis of the emerging economic thinking of his time. It is mostly known due to the idea of **The Invisible Hand**, which means that people will unintentionally improve their community through the pursuit of their own wants and needs.

DAS KAPITAL - KARL MARX

Das Kapital is a political-economic treatise by Karl Marx. The book is a critical analysis of **capitalism** and of the political economy practices during his time. Marx bases his work on that of the classical economists like Adam Smith, David Ricardo, and even Benjamin Franklin.

GENERAL THEORY OF EMPLOYMENT, INTEREST AND MONEY -JOHN MAYNARD KEYNES

The General Theory of Employment, Interest and Money is generally considered to be the masterwork of the English economist John Maynard Keynes. To a great extent, it created the terminology of **modern macroeconomics**. The book ushered in a new age of economic thinking, referred to as the "**Keynesian Revolution**."

Bank Regulations

Since the failure of hundreds of banks during the great depression, the **solvency** of commercial banks has become a responsibility of government. **Demand deposits** are insured by agencies of the government so a depositor is protected from losing assets if a bank should fail. Of course, the major objective of banking regulations is to prevent failures. To maintain the integrity of the banking system, federal and state governments have required commercial banks to follow certain rules and regulations. The most important of these requirements is to ensure banks reserve a certain percentage of their demand deposits as a reserve asset, ensuring that banks do not overextend themselves with loans. Today, only transaction deposits are subject to this rule. This regulation protects depositors against bank insolvency, as does the federal government's insurance plans. The Federal Reserve imposes capital guidelines for commercial banks and savings banks, which provide regulations on certain types of loans. These guidelines are risk-based and protect banks from making poor decisions on a borrower's ability to repay the loan.

Savings

Technically, in economic theory, disposable income is either **consumed** or **saved**. The amount left over when goods and services have been purchased by consumers is considered to be savings. Other categories of savings include corporations' retained earnings and a government surplus. The definition of the term *savings* is subject to various interpretations. Individuals who repay loans of any kind rather than consuming the income are really saving. Interest paid on loans is not savings, but must be counted as income by those who receive the interest. A differentiation must be made between saving, which is to increase assets, and savings, which is one element of a person's total net worth. To save is an activity that results in additional net worth as a separate category. Although this may seem to be a differentiation without a difference, the terms have separate meanings in economic analysis and should be understood in economic terms.

Investments

Investment and savings are two sides of the same coin. If a decision is made to save, the opportunity cost of consumption is sacrificed. Savings can be utilized to **reinvest** in land, capital improvements, and equipment. This type of saving increases the total capita and promotes economic expansion. Savings does not automatically equal **investment**, because both of these decisions are made by different entities in an economy and often for different purposes. It is possible to save yet not increase investment, which can result in a decline in demand, which further leads to increased unemployment, reduction in production, and a business cycle that can lead to recession or depression. This has been named the **paradox of thrift**, because saving more would seem to be a positive spur to the economy, while in many cases it is not. However, when investment increases over savings, aggregate demand is stimulated, and the business cycle may turn toward expansion.

Other Meanings of Investment in Aspects of Finance and Economics

Although investment has a technical meaning in economic theory, it has several other definitions that apply to aspects of finance and economics. In everyday language, we speak of investment as a **speculation** for future gain. Common types of investments are stocks, bonds, government securities, mutual funds, insurance policies, commodities, and real estate. Markets exist in many forms for various types of investments. **Formal exchanges** are the rule in security investing, examples including the New York Stock Exchange and the American Stock Exchange. Investments such as stocks and bonds may provide income in interest and dividends and offer the promise of **appreciation**. Less tangible markets exist for countless items, such as coins, stamps, and markets for professional athletes. Trading in **securities** has become much easier through internet buying and selling. Investment clubs are common in society, and colleges and universities allow students to manage funds as part of their training.

Interest Rates

There are several ways to view interest rates in economics. Interest is the cost of using money in formal analysis. It is the cost of using **capital**. Keynes felt that **interest rates** did not affect saving or investment, as had been believed by classical economists. Classical economics taught that interest rates would adjust toward equilibrium and directly influence savings and investment decisions. As in most areas of economics, the **demand** for and the **supply** of money determine interest rates. The rate of interest will fluctuate depending on many economic variables. Finance employs the term *interest rates* to designate a charge for borrowing money. Interest may also be considered a return on an investment, the interest rate determining the return. It is actually a rate of return on a capital investment. An investor rents money and is charged a percentage of the value of the investment as the cost of borrowing.

Transfer Payments

A transfer payment in economic jargon is any transfer of money from one element of an economy to another, in which there is no expected reciprocal return. Examples of **transfer payments** abound in an economy. Social security transfers, disability and unemployment benefits, and any payment from a government agency for which the recipient does nothing are all forms of transfer payments. Scholarships and interest-free loans are also transfer payments. Transfer payments can also flow between levels of government. Federal disaster relief, subsidies of all kinds, and direct transfers of monies for a multitude of purposes fall into the category of transfer payments. Even state and local taxes are transfer payments in the sense that they are paid by businesses and individuals without getting anything in direct return. Of course, many of the state and municipal functions are providing an indirect return to taxpayers in the form of essential services rendered.

Standard of Deferred Payments

In any transaction, there must be a currency or commodity that is generally accepted as a means of settling debt. **Deferred payment** for a current transaction to be settled later are guided by the standard used at the time. Historically, gold and silver were used as the standard of deferred payments, because they had intrinsic value and everyone could agree on their worth. When the gold standard was in effect, all currencies were guaranteed to be exchanged at a **fixed rate**. In modern economics, the strongest currencies usually serve as the standard of deferred payment. Today, the United States dollar and the European Union's euro are considered the most reliable standard of deferred payment. Illegal transactions rarely allow deferred payments, but if they do, compensation may be made in gold or diamonds, whose store of value is unquestioned. The instability of money at a given time makes the deferred standard of payment more important.

International Monetary Fund

The **international financial network** is a huge and complex array of associations and organizations representing governments, businesses, and individuals. This includes a bewildering number of markets featuring ever-changing exchange rates and fluctuating conditions in the world's economy. Overseeing and monitoring this system is the **International Monetary Fund**. The IMF stands by as a consultant and watchdog over exchange markets and the resulting balance of payments account of participating countries. The IMF is governed by 190 member countries, joining in a cooperative effort to control international markets and avoid financial instability. The institution has grown dramatically since its inception when only 44 countries were included in the charter. Presently, the IMF provides an important role in helping developing nations gain stable economies. Increased membership and the problems of new countries such as those created with the breakup of the Soviet Union have made the role of the IMF an increasingly important one in the world.

Criticisms

As may have been anticipated, the **International Monetary Fund** has become an object of criticism since its charter. One accusation is that the IMF has been partial toward countries that have friendly relations with the United States and other Western powers. Liberal and radical critics accuse the IMF of supporting countries with dictatorships and ignoring complaints regarding civil liberties and human rights in these nations. Defenders of the IMF respond that the organization is an economic group, not a political one. They contend that before a democracy or republic can flourish, it must have a stable economy. The debate continues with liberal politicians supporting the proactive policies of the IMF in stabilizing economies, while more conservative observers feel that supply-side policy would allow the economies of developing nations to grow unimpeded by government intervention. The tendency of the IMF to promote currency devaluation is particularly aggravating to conservative economists and politicians alike.

The World Bank

History

The World Bank was chartered in 1944, when the post-World War II devastation of economies was a major global concern. The organization addressed the problems of rebuilding the economies of Western Europe and providing stability for international investment in those countries (as well as other developing nations). In recent decades, the **World Bank** has become an active participant in reducing poverty and promoting economic growth in **third-world countries**. Included in the economic support is the improvement of education, farming, and manufacturing technology. The major financial tool of the World Bank is to provide funds through **loans** to these countries. The loans usually carry a much lower interest rate than what normally would be charged. The World Bank is actually an association of five separate but related agencies working toward a common goal. It is highly regarded as an organization of integrity by economists and governments alike.

Goals

The work of the World Bank is to provide financial and consulting support for **developing countries**. The problems of dire poverty and famine are common in these countries, and the World Bank is active in attempting to solve these problems. It's tools are primarily financial, but the World Bank serves as an economic resource for financial planning for these countries. Funds are loaned at preferable interest rates to build or repair infrastructure of countries, as well as promote social and economic reforms. Environmental issues are important to the World Bank in making loans and supporting third-world countries. A new emphasis on reducing poverty has influenced recent policy at the World Bank. This includes the advocacy for individual businesses to rebuild flagging economies. Broader goals have been related to the improvement of the standard of living through the promotion of reduced pollution, education, and the creation of entities capable of sustainable growth over time.

Criticisms

Although the World Bank has a generally good reputation in global economics, it is not without its critics. The crux of these concerns is that many of their programs include provisions that alter the structure of the society and rob it of its **autonomy**. Almost always, the World Bank promotes economic liberation from archaic practices, which are sometimes deeply ingrained in the society of a country. These policies often reduce the power of a nation in managing its own economy, in the interest of promoting the general welfare.

Another related criticism of the World Bank is its liberal and progressive political stance. The Bank often requires countries to accept certain conditions as a requisite for financial aid. Sometimes, critics argue that these requirements include reforms not appropriate for unstable governments and countries in conflict. The influence of the United States is often thought to be excessive, and this causes policy that would favor American economic and political interests. Examples include the introduction of foreign businesses to compete with local industries.

Problems with Equating GDP Per Capita and Economic Well-Being

Several economic factors may interfere with equating GDP per capita with individual well-being. A significant allocation of assets is used to combat the negative effects of economic growth such as the destruction of natural habitats and air and water pollution. Economic growth increases such **intangibles** as the increase in commuting, which affects quality of life. Perhaps most importantly, GDP does not account for a significant amount of **domestic production,** such as child-raising and homemaking. The money equivalents for these tasks are omitted from the GDP calculation. There are numerous markets that are left out of GDP, including black markets, criminal activity, and alternative economies. There is also no provision in GDP for volunteer activity, "do it yourself" tasks such as home improvements and landscape management. All of these economic activities are omitted from the formal measurement of per capita GDP and fail to give an accurate picture of individual well-being.

Unemployment in Capitalism

Unemployment in a free market situation occurs only in **capitalistic** economic systems. In Fascism, Socialism, and Communism, the factors of production, including labor, are under the direct control of the **state**. Historically, precapitalist societies such as feudalism formed the basis for the economy. In this case, the serfs were all employed (if able) by mandate of the lords. More primitive societies such as tribes view the entire group as part of one family and take responsibility for ensuring all are cared for adequately. Debate continues on the necessary and appropriate action of governments in curbing unemployment. Liberal and welfare economists often call for a more active role for government in increasing employment, while more conservative analysts feel government intervention exacerbates the problem by its interference. Laws forbidding strikes and layoffs are cited as inappropriate government action to solve unemployment.

Economic Indicators

Business or economic indicators are specific measurements that are used to predict the future course of the economy. They are used as analytical tools to measure and forecast economic activity and future behavior of the economy. Common **economic indicators** are indexes, compilations of data, summaries of economic activity in a period of time, and statistics measuring the level of consumption, investment, savings, and unemployment in the economy. Fluctuations in the money supply and industrial output are important indicators. Measurements for inflation, retail sales, and stock market prices provide supporting data. The National Bureau of Economic Research, whose prime interest is in predicting business cycles, provides many of the important economic indicators used for forecasting. When an indicator occurs behind economic activity, it is called a **lagging indicator**. Indicators current with economic activity are known as **coincident indicators**.

Economic Policy Goals and Tools

Governments and economies usually set **goals** for their economic plans and policy decisions. Goals may be short-term or long-term, and they tend to focus on big-picture elements such as inflation control, employment levels, and economic growth rates. These policy goals are implemented with economic tools that include monetary and fiscal policy, increases or decreases in government spending, international trade practices, regulation of labor markets, and many additional methods.

Often, goals are not exclusively economic, as with defense and other areas of the general welfare. A government must determine which short-term goals are most important to its policy. It may be impossible to reduce inflation while promoting more employment at the same time. Governments are usually more successful with a few short-term goals that work with each other to affect long-term goals. A consistent policy approach to economic problems is essential to achieve economic goals.

Chapter Quiz

Ready to see how well you retained what you just read? Scan the QR code to go directly to the chapter quiz interface for this study guide. If you're using a computer, simply visit the online resources page at **mometrix.com/resources719/apmicroeconom** and click the Chapter Quizzes link.

SUBSIDIES

In economics, a subsidy is a unilateral transfer of money, usually by a government institution, artificially supporting the price of a commodity based on the importance of that good to the general welfare. **Subsidies** take various forms, including direct cash payments, letters of credit, or tax incentives. Subsidies guarantee the producer a better price than may be obtained on the open market. They correspondingly reduce the consumer price but at a cost to the free operation of the market. Subsidies skew demand and supply curves and encourage consumers to spend rather than save. This hurts the economy and the consumers by causing overconsumption because of an artificially lower price. Subsidies have historically been used for agricultural products, particularly under governments attempting to increase income to producers. Subsidies were used heavily during the New Deal and Fair Deal to help selected groups in the economy.

TRADE BETWEEN NATIONS

Commerce between nations, the trading of products and service functions from one country to another, is called **international trade**. Trade between countries was very limited in the premodern era. As the capabilities for shipping and transport increased, so did the opportunities for international commerce. Today, it constitutes a significant portion of many countries' economies. The rise of companies doing business in many countries has contributed to the increase of international trade. The term "**globalization**" has come to mean the spreading network of economic ties throughout the world. International trade is used as a political as well as economic strategy in relations between nations. As countries seek new markets in order to grow and prosper, international commerce is an ideal avenue for economic growth. **Tariff policy** is another weapon used in geopolitics as nations strive to prosper in an increasingly competitive world. Economic success for many individual firms depends on their ability to develop international markets for their goods and services.

POTENTIAL ECONOMIC RISKS IN INTERNATIONAL TRADE

The primary risks in international trade are **economic** in nature. Care must be taken in international commerce to accurately assess the economic stability of the buyer. Trade partners must have confidence in the liquidity of their counterparts and be assured that the buyer has the continued means to meet his obligations. This confidence fosters an atmosphere where international commerce can grow and flourish. Countries must believe that they have not lost control of their economic destiny by trading freely. Another related area of concern is the **geopolitical arena**. Economic policy is a powerful tool that can be used as a political weapon. Concerns about trading with potential enemies as well as possible confiscation during periods of international strife are real. Firms may become dependent on certain licenses to engage in international business, and fear the revocation of these agreements. The uncertainty of foreign exchange rates and stability of trading partners' economies remain realistic concerns in today's global economy.

BALANCE OF TRADE

Every country hopes to have a positive **balance of trade.** This means they have sold more goods and services abroad than they have purchased. Such a positive balance of trade (called a **surplus**) indicates a strong economy with good international markets. Conversely, a **negative balance of trade** (called a **deficit**) can indicate some fundamental weakness in a country's ability to profitably engage in international commerce. Trade restrictions, including tariffs and other regulations, can weaken a country's trading position. Widely fluctuating exchange rates may cast uncertainty on the wisdom of trading with a particular country. Social and political environments have a direct effect on international commerce. Basic economic indicators such as inflation, price levels, and aggregate demand and supply all have a bearing on the balance of payments. Ultimately, it is the totality of all these issues that may determine the success of a country in international business.

Utility Function and Neoclassical Economics

Neoclassical economists consider the **utility function** paramount in most economic and non-economic choices of individuals and states. This includes both short-term and long-term economics. This theory of economic behavior extends to decisions made daily by consumers. What to consume and at what cost are the driving forces of microeconomics. Understanding that consumption choices involve opportunity costs is implicit in the economic choices made. **Neoclassical economists** tend to favor what has been termed supply-side economics, focusing on providing incentives to individuals and businesses rather than attempting to manipulate demand. **Monetarism** attempts to influence economic activity and growth through increasing or decreasing the money supply in an economy. Proponents of this philosophy tend to reject direct government intervention in the economy.

Modeling and Economic Reasoning

The development of a methodology and logistical framework for discussion and argument has been an important step in the development of economics as a science. Modern economics has utilized new information gathering and processing technologies that expedite and organize the compilation of economic information. Much more detailed data is now available as the raw material for economic methodology. The application of **modeling** to economics has provided a framework for the application of the scientific method to economics, to study economic behavior and test hypotheses. Modeling allows the creation of artificial relationships to measure and manipulate economic activities. Models mirror the real world of economics and provide an opportunity for economists to systematically study economic relationships. As more sophisticated methods of study have evolved, the application of mathematics to economics, termed *econometrics*, has yielded more accurate and useful information in economic methodology.

Microeconomic Theory

The development of economic theory as it relates to individual units in a society is called **microeconomics**. These units may be individuals, firms, labor forces, resource pools, and consumers. The behavior of both people and businesses is included in microeconomics. The term itself means "small-scale" economics. Microeconomics questions how the activities of small units in an economy interact, and theorizes about the implications of such transactions. The utilization of scarce resources by individuals and firms is a central topic in microeconomics. Models of the marketplace where households and commercial companies interact and trade are key components in microeconomics. Economic activity is sometimes viewed as a process between corporations, businesses, and individuals. This process illustrates the mechanisms of a market economy when studied from small individual units within that economy. Relationships between scarce assets, such as natural resources, money, labor, and the factors of production are all easily visualized from the individual level of economics.

Principles of Supply and Demand

A competitive market is composed of buyers and sellers engaged in trade in an organized manner. The price and the number of products sold are determined by the **supply** of and **demand** for the goods or services. **Microeconomics** is the study of these market factors to understand and predict market activity. A central tenet of the market is the rise in price when demand exceeds supply of a good or service. However, when supply exceeds demand for a good or service, the price will fall. The constant flux of demand, supply, and price always tends toward **equilibrium**, when supply and demand equal each other. In real economic systems, this point is rarely reached, and if so, only briefly. In a complex economy where there are endless choices to be made, demand and supply only occasionally reach an equilibrium. Elements of economic choice and the opportunity cost of such choices make it very difficult for demand and supply to be equal for a particular good or service.

Market Equilibrium

The condition of market equilibrium is achieved when demand for a good or service equals the amount of that product made available by suppliers. Any organized market tends to work toward a state of **equilibrium**, as the forces of supply and demand fluctuate over time. Shortages may occur, causing increased demand and higher prices. The higher prices will reduce demand, causing prices to drop as the market moves toward equilibrium. The equilibrium point is rarely, if ever, actually attained, since the endless changes in supply, demand, and fluctuating prices create some imbalance between supply and demand. Despite this reality, it is important to note that a free market is always working toward this equilibrium state. The economic behavior of buyers and sellers will move the market in the direction of balance between demand and supply.

Results of Shortage

When a good or service is demanded in excess of the ability of the supplier to meet this demand, a **shortage** will occur. A shortage will drive the **demand** for a product or service up, and **prices** will rise. Shortages can be artificially manufactured by suppliers to manipulate the market. An example of this occurred in the 1970s when OPEC chose to limit the production of oil in order to increase demand, and thus raise prices. This proved to be an effective strategy, as Americans who depended on gasoline increased demand and prices rose because of the shortage. When OPEC increased the production of oil after political pressure was applied, supplies of gasoline returned to normal and prices fell. The market again moved toward equilibrium as the artificial manipulation of the supply of oil ended. This episode drove home the point that to depend on a few suppliers of a necessary product leaves consumers open to manipulated shortages.

Markets and Perfectly Competitive Markets

Markets may be located physically in particular places, such as a produce market, or may be intangible, such as a market for fine art. All markets operate under an implied agreement between buyers and sellers on trading for goods and services at specified but fluctuating prices. Markets provide the laboratory where economic theory and practice may be observed and studied. Anywhere that goods are offered for sale and buyers exist, a **market** is said to be present. A **specialized** type of market is one in which all products are the same and everyone has equal access to market information. Such a market is said to be **perfectly competitive** when it reaches a significant size. The size must be large enough that individual units of the market (buyers and sellers) are unable to determine the price of the goods or services by themselves. In such a market, perfect competition may be said to exist. Practically, perfectly competitive markets are uncommon, due to a myriad of factors that affect a given market.

Price and Price Theory

A free market depends on a system of value to measure the scope and action of an economic system. **Price** is the traditional measurement of value between sellers and buyers in a market. **Price theory** measures the relationship between prices and other economic variables in a market economy. Price theory has demonstrated the importance of prices on both demand and supply in economic analysis. The demand for resources is a derived demand, based on demand for the products that require the resources for their production. The greater the demand for the final products of the resources the higher the price of those resources. Thus, resources are priced just as goods and services are priced: according to the demand and supply for the resources. It follows that the price of final goods and services depends in large part on the price of the resources needed to supply the final product.

Price Discrimination

When a supplier of the same goods and services uses a multitier price schedule to sell to different buyers, **price discrimination** exists. Airlines provide a prime example, selling services for the same flight at many different prices depending on the purchase date, age of the buyer, days traveled, and many other factors. Price discrimination is an economic strategy designed to increase economic profitability in a mixed market. It does not mean unfair or illegal manipulation of prices. Sometimes, a **reverse price discrimination** occurs, when a supplier charges the same price to different buyers, although the costs of the supplier to do so differ. One would imagine that price discrimination could only occur if a supplier held a monopoly; however, in a complex economy with so many pricing factors and decisions at work, discrimination in pricing occurs almost everywhere. Sometimes, this variation in prices can help lower prices for consumers, but this is not always the case.

Commercial Airlines

As everyone who purchases tickets on an airline knows, price discrimination is rampant. The same flight from San Francisco to New York may offer a bewildering number of prices based on such factors as:

- Length (number of days) of the trip.
- Age of the traveler.
- Day of the week traveled.
- Purchase date of the ticket.
- Number of stops en route to destination.
- Special fares and discounts not available to all travelers.
- Class of service offered on the flight.
- Flexibility of ticket.

Airlines sell into both business and vacation travel markets and often change their prices significantly. The success of online travel agencies has highlighted the price discrimination for airline tickets. A quick glance at one of these websites will show multiple examples of airline price discrimination.

Adam Smith and Value

Value is the key economic element that drives many business decisions. Unfortunately, **value** may be difficult to define, as it means different things to different people. It is, however, the measurement by which utility, or want-satisfying power, may be defined. Some classical economists, including **Adam Smith**, tied **labor** to value, postulating that true value was the amount of work it takes to produce a good or service for sale. Although this is one legitimate manner in which to measure value, it is not the only one. An exception would be the relative ease of "making" emeralds, compared to the complexity of producing aircraft. The element of **scarcity** is also a vital component of the value of a good or service. Some market theorists claim that **price** itself tells the value of a good or service. They believe that countless economic variables are factored into determining a price for a specific good or service, and this price equals the value. In some sense, value is a determinant of the individual's belief in the want-satisfying power of any good or service.

Competition Policy

Each state has enacted laws designed to control **competition practices** of businesses. These laws cover many aspects of competition but are generally designed to ensure competition is not impeded. They protect small businesses and consumers against the possible abuses of oligopolies and monopolies. Each nation that encourages **free trade** has its own laws to protect competition. However, the adequacy of these laws, and the stringency with which they are enforced, varies widely among countries of the world. Perhaps the United States is most vigilant in these areas, having scores of antitrust laws on the books to protect competition. In America, the **Department of Justice** monitors all proposed mergers and acquisitions to insure they will not significantly reduce competition. They have the power to deny such mergers and takeovers if they feel the public interest is negatively affected. The government has the ability to force large monopolistic conglomerates to break up if they unfairly control markets.

Welfare Economics

The analysis of income distribution and its consequences is called **welfare economics**. This field uses microeconomic theory to measure the effectiveness of the economic system in improving the general welfare. Welfare economics takes as its starting point the individual, the most basic component of an economy. Careful analysis of individual economic behavior yields a much clearer understanding of the macroeconomic picture of an economy. How well the wants and needs of a society are met may be termed **social welfare**. It may be viewed as the aggregate sum of the welfare of all individuals in a society. Welfare can be measured by dollars or income, or more generally in terms of individual economic satisfaction. Two major components of welfare economics are **economic efficiency**, which considers the total wealth of a society, and **income distribution**, which focuses on how the wealth is allocated throughout the economy. Both are key indicators of the general welfare.

Price Elasticity

When a price is changed, there will be a change in the demand for the goods and services. The rate at which demand falls or rises is called the **price elasticity of demand**. This measurement is usually formulated as a ratio of the changing price and the change in demand. If a price is raised by 20% and demand falls by 20%, the ratio between them is the price elasticity of demand. Normally, any rise in price will decrease the demand for the goods and services offered. Any decrease in price should raise demand, barring other external factors. This theory of price elasticity works best as a model, because in the real economic world, there are a huge number of variables that affect price and demand. Usually, businesses will test these variables to determine how much a price change will by itself affects demand.

Cross Elasticity of Demand and Income Elasticity of Demand

If the demand of a good or service is affected by the change in price of a different good or service, **cross elasticity** of demand is at work. This is most often expressed as a ratio between the **change in demand** for the first good as the price of the second good fluctuates. An example of this would be the change in demand for subway tickets in New York if the price of each ticket were to be doubled. The ratio between the drop in demand for use of the subway and the amount of the price increase would be the cross elasticity of demand. The demand for a good or service is related to the income of prospective buyers of the good or service. Changes in the income of prospective consumers are measured in a ratio to the change in demand caused by the income change. If the income of a buyer pool increases 10% and the demand for the product increases 10%, that ratio (1:1) is the income elasticity of demand.

PRICE ELASTICITY OF SUPPLY

The price of a good or service directly affects the quantity of supply of that good or service. The ratio between the price increase or decrease and the amount of the good or service supplied is called the **price elasticity of supply**. For example, a rise in the price of carrots will cause an increase in the supply of carrots as farmers produce more of that crop to increase profits. This price elasticity of supply is expressed as a ratio between the increase or decrease in price and the increase or decrease of supply. If the price of carrots rises on the open market by 10% and the supply of carrots increases by 10%, the price elasticity of supply would be expressed as the ratio between these changes (1:1). Note that inventories of goods already produced will be a factor in determining the price elasticity of supply. Over the long run, economists equate goods produced with goods supplied.

SURPLUS

A **consumer surplus** arises when prices fall and buyers realize extra savings, which go into a surplus of buying power for purchasers. If, for any number of economic factors, suppliers are able to sell at higher prices than they would ordinarily obtain, a **supplier surplus** exists. In many areas, particularly commodities and farm products, governments intervene, which may cause an artificial surplus. This government intervention usually takes the form of subsidies of some kind and often represents the government holding a significant surplus itself. Taxes are another area of government intervention that can cause a surplus. When all the existing surpluses in an economy are aggregated, the sum may be called the **total surplus**. Welfare economics uses this figure when they consider a new policy or examine an existing one.

INDIVIDUAL DEMAND CURVES

A demand by consumers or buyers is analyzed based on the ability of any good or service to satisfy the needs of that group. When all economic considerations are in play, including the price of a good or service and the amount supplied, consumers will, in general, choose the economic decisions that most fulfill their wants and needs. When all of these individual preferences are analyzed, the total pattern will represent **aggregate demand curves**. Although each individual will operate to fulfill his or her needs as a separate unit, the aggregate of the total economy may differ. Social programs, tax incentives, and transfer payments will change the pattern of wealth distribution for the entire economy. Society, as an entity, may have a different aggregate demand than any individual. Since there is always a broad spectrum of wants and needs in any given society, the market cannot give a "greatest good for the greatest number" with any certainty.

THEORIES OF VALUE

Placing value on goods and services has been a problem concerning economists for centuries. Many scholastic and scientific arguments of the reformation period focused on the definition of value. The classical argument of value is illustrated in the "diamond-water paradox." It is pointed out in comparisons of these goods that water is essential to life and either free or available at a low price, while diamonds are a very expensive, unnecessary luxury. Classical economic thinkers claimed that value could only be measured as the cost of production of the product. The difficulty and expense of making a good available imputed it with intrinsic value. Both Adam Smith and David Ricardo promulgated this **theory of value**. Another school of thought on determining value stated that the value of anything was completely subjective; nothing is valuable in and of itself, and only the perceived value imputed by the consumer is valid. This school, called the **subjective theory of value**, asserted itself through the 20th century.

Efficient Market Theory

Capital markets work under a different set of principles than other markets. The market for stocks and bonds is an example of a capital market. Fama's "**efficient market theory**" attempts to describe the forces that operate in capital markets. According to this theory, the price of an equity security or bond is determined by an overall objective assessment of its perceived value after all information regarding the security is available and taken into account. This is only accurate in theory, because it assumes all information about the security is accurate (very rarely true) and that all individuals receive the information at the same time (almost never true). Additional assumptions are made that all relevant information arises spontaneously and the market is broad enough that no small group of individuals can manipulate the price. Sometimes called the "**random walk theory**," it claims that any attempt to forecast market prices based on mathematical calculations or market analysis is futile.

Market Failure

The term *market failure* has several definitions in economics. At the most basic level, it means the market is unable to provide a stable trading framework for the distribution of goods and services to the buyers. In this case, the market does not truly function under the economic definition of a trading exchange. Another way of viewing **market failure** is the common situation where the market is so grossly inefficient it simply malfunctions. Social welfare economists would deem any market that did not place the good of the society above all other factors as a failure. In trying to understand the mechanics of market failure, economists have created models to study the phenomenon. They believe market failure is often the result of errors in pricing based on faulty market research. Inaccurate information in setting prices can be a major cause of failure. Perhaps the major cause of market failure is the failure to adequately understand the nuances of the particular market involved.

Economic Rent

In economics, *economic rent* is a technical term that defines the ratio between the cost of a factor of production and the revenue yielded by that factor. The utilization of each factor of production involves an opportunity cost that must be evaluated by a company. Choices the firm makes will decide on the optimal use of these factors in light of income received. A company must make decisions that select the processes which best optimize the productivity of that firm. A technical distinction may be made between **economic rent** and profits, because business entities often own manufacturing and capital equipment and derive multiple benefits from them. **Profit** is a more narrow concept, which may be calculated easily by subtracting business costs from business income. The two may be substantially different, depending on the organization of a company, ownership of capital goods, and the method of accounting used. Economic rent is a more theoretical term, while profit and loss are practical indicators of the success or failure of a business.

Economies of Scale

Economies of scale is an economic concept that measures the effects of the increase in production of a given product. **Economies of scale** refers to the changing variables that must occur when production is increased or decreased. The goal of this economic measurement is to determine the most ideal size of a company to maximize productivity and decrease inefficiency. Many factors enter into this concept, including the available labor force, size of the physical plant necessary, cost and availability of raw materials, and managerial expertise to mix and balance these elements most effectively. Ultimately, economies of scale are used to increase productivity and profit, the two measurements that are vital to the success of a firm. **Diseconomies of scale** indicate when production changes have reached a point where they are detrimental to the firm. This can be valuable information as companies plan production strategies and levels.

Economies of scope are primarily concerned with the planning and implementation of product mix as a strategy of marketing and distribution. Economies of scale deal with the amounts of goods and services supplied, while economies of scope are more concerned with the types and numbers of different products the firm markets. An example would be a candy manufacturer deciding to introduce a new variation of an existing candy bar. Marketing and distribution channels would remain the same, name recognition would be present, and the product would fit nicely into the overall product concept of the firm. Should the company decide to add shoes to its line, diseconomies of scope become evident. Marketing strategy and distribution agencies would be different, as would packaging, storing, and shipping the final product. Such diseconomies of scope place major barriers in the path of product expansion into new and uncharted markets.

Problems of Oversized Firms

Firms that become too large may encounter problems that impair their efficiency and productivity. The usual result of **oversized firms** is an increase in cost resulting in decreased profits. Several problems are common when a business grows too quickly or reaches an unwieldy size. Many times, rapid growth causes duplication of essential production or marketing functions. Overall communication can slow, with the result of a firm that may be less responsive to changes in the economy or their markets. As firms grow, a certain inertia may set in: an unwillingness to change outmoded business practices. Increased size almost always results in more managers who are further removed from the vital operations of the company. Sometimes, a company will end up competing with itself in some areas. Companies can grow so quickly they lose touch with their customers and fail to accurately assess changing markets. Rapid growth can be desirable but almost always compounds a firm's problems, and often creates new ones.

Top-Heavy Companies

As a company experiences rapid growth, the percentage of middle and upper management usually grows. **Managers** serve a vital function in shaping company policy, supervising operations, and planning for the future. However, managers rarely increase the productivity of a firm. Typically, managers who supervise and do not perform vital company operations will lower the efficiency of an organization. As firms develop over time, managers, who may be viewed as the most unproductive part of the organization, increase in numbers and influence. Sometimes, managers also have dual roles as line workers who directly impact the vital operations of a firm. This is an ideal but uncommon situation. Managers who only supervise add only an intangible and incremental asset to the firm. It is not unusual to see corporations with layers of relatively unproductive **middle and upper management**. This almost always works to the detriment of the company.

Solutions to Outsized Companies

Breaking a large unwieldy company into smaller, more responsive units is often an excellent solution to the **overgrowth** of a company. Firms will sometimes assess their operating divisions and decide to retain only the most profitable ones. Others will be sold or eliminated. Failure of a company that declares bankruptcy sometimes forces such action. Hostile takeovers of a business will almost always result in the elimination of unprofitable centers and the reorganization of the entire company. Government intervention is sometimes the catalyst for the reorganization of a firm that has become too monopolistic. All of these solutions are undesirable when forced upon a company from an outside source. A thoughtful and resourceful firm will take a proactive position in solving **growth problems**. It is much better for a company to position itself to take advantage of growth rather than have changes imposed upon it.

Costs and Revenues

Costs and revenues are the two determinants of income, the most common measuring tools for assessing business success. Firms incur **fixed costs**, which are constant and do not depend on that amount of production. Examples would be physical plants and heavy equipment, which must be paid for even if production is zero. **Variable costs** are tied directly to the production of finished goods and services. As more goods are produced, variable costs rise. Examples of variable costs are raw materials used in the production process, extra labor needed in peak production periods, and additional capital if expansion is needed. **Revenue** is the aggregate amount of income that the firms receive from any source. The most common source of income is the **sale of deeds and services**, but additional monies may be gleaned from transfer payments, investment return, and additional investment by owners. Corporations have the ability to raise money through issuing additional stock or floating bonds at attractive interest rates, as well as using venture capital to increase revenue.

Profit Maximization

The usual goal of any business concern is the **maximization of profits**. Sole business owners, partnerships, and corporations all face this problem. There are a number of common strategies for increasing profits for these concerns. The most important for any type of business is to find the amount of production of finished goods at a certain price that guarantees the best return. One approach is to cut costs to a level to produce an optimum profit. This involves determining at what point the minimum input will result in an optimal level of per-unit products. This would be a level of profit maximization. Another tactic is to increase sales in an attempt to improve the profit picture. A flaw in this approach is that as units produced increase, variable costs also go up. Profit maximization is determined by a myriad of economic factors, some beyond the control of an individual firm. Variables that can be determined by the firm can position it to take advantage of favorable economic conditions. Maximizing opportunities in any economic environment is the challenge for an individual company.

Elements Involved in Pricing

Pricing is an essential element in marketing. It is a sophisticated business practice and one that may cause a product's success or failure. The simple definition of **pricing** is the **assignment of monetary amounts** to goods and services sold by the company. Complexities of this process include varying prices to different customers, special price promotions, determining the price based on fluctuating variable costs, special quantity pricing, incentive pricing for multiple orders of dissimilar products, and accurately assessing the price the market will bear. Pricing must be based on accurate market research, which provides insights into the buying habits of the potential market. Clear objectives for pricing must be set, and knowledge of the competition's pricing policies is critical. Decisions must be made on volume or bulk pricing, pricing for international sales, zone pricing (varying prices in different geographical areas), the use of discounts, and the understanding of the market's price sensitivity. All of those factors (and several others) will determine the price charged for a particular good or service.

Process of Setting Goals in Pricing

Prices are determined to fulfill several purposes, the main one being a sufficient price to ensure sales that will attain the **financial goals** of the firm. The price must also be realistic when compared to the marketplace and competition. It would be an error to price a new candy bar at $1.00 if competing bars of similar size sell for $0.75. Price must also fit into a company's overall marketing plan, which will include channels of distribution, manufacturing requirements, and storing and shipping facilities. The quality of the product in the market (high-end/low-end), planned promotional and overall marketing strategies, and the effectiveness of the sales force all play a part in pricing. In general, prices should reflect the most that customers are willing to pay for it. This will usually result in the most income per unit. The **effective price** of a product is monies the firm obtains from sales of goods and services after special pricing strategies (promotions, incentives, and discounts) are considered.

Special Pricing Strategies

There are several special pricing strategies used in different phases of the life of the product. When a product is introduced, an introductory lower price may induce people to try the product. The goal is to secure a market base and then raise the price to a more appropriate level. Sometimes a price is applied that is near the highest level of the pricing scale. This is intended to underscore the quality of the product and is sometimes called premium pricing. Retailers sometimes use artificially lower prices on some products to attract customers in the hope they will make additional purchases. This is called **"loss leader" pricing**. **Demand pricing** is any pricing tactic that is based on market research into consumer demand for the product. Consumers tend to believe a higher price (within reason) relates to a higher-quality product. Products may be sold together (bundled) at a special price. Economies of scope, scale, and agglomeration all play an important role in **special pricing strategies**.

Perfect Competition and Monopolistic Competition

There is no such thing as perfect competition in the real world. It exists only as an economic model, describing a theoretical market where the base of producers and consumers is so large that they are unable to influence prices. Ideally, this would lead to a textbook definition of economic efficiency. For **perfect competition** to exist, products are essentially the same, each type being an equal substitute for another. Prices are set by the market, and firms must accept this determination. All businesses must have equal access to existing information, raw materials, and the latest technology. **Monopolistic competition** has a different set of standards. Usually, there are numerous producers and a great number of consumers in any market. No regulations exist to entering or leaving the market, and consumers have more product knowledge and have definite choices between products. These markets give individual companies more influence over their markets. They may raise or lower prices and make adjustments based on the response of the market.

Oligopoly and Oligopsony

When any particular market is controlled by a small group of suppliers, an **oligopoly** is said to exist. In this situation, all suppliers are cognizant of each other's activities. When any one firm makes an economic decision, it will impact the activity of all other firms in the oligopoly. There is a great deal of interaction between members of oligopolies, and planning by any one firm must consider the likely responses of all other members. Oligopolies were very common in certain industries, but antitrust laws have limited their power. In an **oligopsony** market, there are limited numbers of buyers and an unlimited number of sellers. When a relatively small number of businesses are competing to acquire factors of production, this situation is common. Here, buyers will have a competitive advantage and will be aware of each other's economic activity. Sometimes, a situation arises where there are only a few buyers and a few sellers. This unusual situation results in a **bilateral oligopsony**.

Monopoly and Monopsony

When one supplier is the sole seller of a service or product, a **monopoly** is said to exist. There is no competition in a monopolistic economy, as there is only one provider or seller. Usually, in a monopoly, there are no ready substitutes for the products being supplied. Some monopolies are legal in a sense, a prime example being AT&T before it was broken up by government intervention. **Legal monopolies** are common in government agencies and institutions and sometimes exist in specialized private sectors of the economy. Sometimes, an economic phenomenon occurs where there is only a single consumer of a product, and there may be a number of suppliers. This is called **monopsony** and only occurs in specialized industries that have large institutional consumers. **Cartels** differ from monopolies by coordinating the action of a few suppliers to gain economic advantage. Cartels are several firms acting in concert to create an economic advantage. Cartels organize and act as if one business in order to control a finite market.

Monopolistic Competition, Horizontal Monopoly, and Vertical Monopoly

When an industry or portion of an industry is so dominated by a company that it controls the market completely, a **"de facto" monopoly** is said to exist. This condition is sometimes called **monopolistic competition**. The dominance of Microsoft in computer software in the 1980s and '90s created monopolistic competition. The government has intervened at a few points in the past. Sometimes, a large corporation will buy or control smaller firms who are considered competitors and create a **horizontal monopoly**. These companies may have different names and trademarks but still belong to the parent corporation. This type of economic organization is called a horizontal monopoly. A **vertical monopoly** is the control of associated goods and services by one corporation. For example, an oil company may own oil fields, refineries, and distribution channels to retailers in order to control an entire production and marketing flow for a product.

Characteristics of a Monopoly

To qualify as a monopoly, several conditions must exist. Primarily, there is only **one producer or supplier** of a good or service, and attempts for other firms to enter as competitors are discouraged by economic action of the monopoly holder. This action may be based on better or unique technology, patents on products that allow no competition, and the economic realities of trying to enter a market that is controlled by such a dominating economic entity. These actions and others like them are collectively called **blocking the entry** to a monopolistic market. These economic actions may or may not be in restraint of trade. In a monopolistic situation, the product being monopolized usually has **no comparable substitutes or alternatives**. It can have no true competition, forcing consumers to buy from the monopolizing corporation. The company controlling the monopoly can manipulate the price and available supply of the product involved. Artificial shortages can be created that force prices upward.

Business Organizations

Business organizations operate under a bevy of laws and regulations that mandate both their organization and activities. There are a number of types of organization that companies may choose. The most common form of business entity is the **sole proprietorship**. An example of this would be "mom and pop" businesses found everywhere. **Partnerships** bring together two or more individuals as joint owners of a business. There are a number of various types of partnerships that define, limit, and regulate business practices and liabilities. Most familiar is the **corporate** form of business organization. Many familiar United States companies are organized and run as corporations. Besides these more common forms of organization, specialized types of arrangements such as limited liability companies, cooperatives formed by individuals for specific economic purposes, government-owned institutions, and pension funds and credit unions may be found in most economies.

Sole Proprietorship

A privately owned business with one principal owner who operates in his or her own name is called a **sole proprietorship**. Such an organization essentially functions as an individual who incurs any debts or liabilities of the business as personal obligations. For example, a lawsuit against a sole proprietorship that gains a judgment could seek compensation from both the business and the individual. Taxation affects the sole proprietorship much like an individual, in that he or she is taxed on personal and business income. Requirements for accounting and regulations are much simpler for the sole proprietorship type of organization. Individuals owning small businesses may still choose to name their business as they wish and can file for a registered trade name that allows them to do business under that name rather than their own. Even in these cases, the individual remains responsible for the debts and liabilities of his or her business.

Partnerships

Partnerships are business organizations where two or more individuals enter into an agreement to share in the financial proceeds (or losses) of a business in which they have invested resources. **General partners** are fully responsible for all liabilities the partnership incurs to third parties. **Limited partners**, while still liable for debts and obligations of the partnership, have their exposure limited to the extent they are invested in the organization. **Silent partners** are those who take no active role in operating the business, and may or may not be publicly associated with the firm. Partnerships often involve the legal formality of declaring their intention to do business. A formal agreement of partnership may be prepared and a public announcement made of the formation of the partnership, with some jurisdictions requiring partnerships to register and make available their records to the public. These usually include only the terms of the partnership and not financial records.

Limited Partnerships and Limited Liability Partnerships

Generally, a limited partnership operates under the same conditions as a general partnership, with the exception that one or more limited partners join one or more general partners in the organization. **General partners** have all the rights and liabilities of any business owner. **Limited partners** initially make a specific investment of funds to the partnership, and their liability for debts and judgments against the partnership is limited to the amount of their investment. Limited partners have no role in managing the operations of the partnership, except in an advisory capacity. They are, however, required to publicly declare their ownership by various registration procedures. Organizations of professionals, such as physicians, attorneys, and other such groups, often form **Limited Liability Partnerships**, which place various limits on the financial exposure of each partner. Limits and statutes vary between states, but often, partners are protected from liability in a judgment simply because they belong to the organization.

Corporations

The term *corporation* is a legal one, defining the rules and regulations for a business, non-profit organization, or institution to **incorporate**. Governmental entities such as cities and towns may also choose to incorporate. Voluntary associations need not apply for corporate status. **Corporations** often operate as an **individual person** might, with power to make agreements, own land and capital equipment, and participate in business. In a sense, a corporation is a person under the law, and subject to rules and regulations any person must abide by. Additionally, there are specific obligations a corporation must perform, including public registration and other regulations deemed necessary by the state in which the corporation intends to do business. Corporations differ from individuals in some important ways. They cannot cast votes in public elections, nor can they as an entity be imprisoned (although individual members of the corporation could be incarcerated).

Features

Corporations must file formal documents with a state describing the particulars of the **intended corporation**. This includes any stock issues (public or private), the identity of officers of the proposed corporation, and the general rules and operating procedures for the corporation. The laws of the state in which the corporation is licensed regulate its business practices, including many financial restrictions. When stock is issued, shareholders of a corporation may be individuals, institutions, other corporations, or government agencies. If no stock is involved in the corporation, it may still incorporate and often is called a "society," "membership corporation," or other title indicating no stock is outstanding for the corporation. There is usually a board of officers and directors who operate the corporation on behalf of the owners. This board is responsible for the financial affairs of the company, as well as making policy and human resource decisions, including the appointment or election of the major officers of the firm.

Types

When the term corporation is used to describe a business organization, what immediately comes to mind is a business that issues common or preferred stock that is publicly traded on an organized stock exchange. More accurately, this type of business organization is called a **public corporation**. Many large and familiar firms fall into this category. Privately held corporations, known as **closed corporations**, are much more common. These entities may issue stock to a select number of officers, but there is no public trading on any organized market. Both individuals and companies may be the stockholders of these closed corporations. They usually include only a relatively small number of stockholders. Some corporations have expanded (or were originally organized) to do business all over the world. The phenomenon of globalization has witnessed the increasing number and economic power of what we now term *multinational corporations*. These companies are regulated in each country in which they do business. Some are separately incorporated in multiple countries.

Economic Theory of Pareto Efficiency

An important economic theory that studies the effects of alternative choices in resource allocation is **Pareto efficiency**. This is an important analytical tool in modern economics. First posited by the Italian economist **Vilfredo Pareto**, it seeks to study the level of economic efficiency determined by the distribution of income. Simply stated, if a change in the allocation of resources improves the economic condition of one individual or group without hurting another individual or group, this is called **Pareto improvement**. Pareto efficiency is a sophisticated economic analytical tool that incorporates aspects of mathematics, social science, and engineering. If an economy is proved to be Pareto efficient, then no individual or group within that economy can be improved by switching allocations of resources without degrading the economic condition of another individual or group in that economy. In this case, no shift of resources will benefit the society.

Abram Bergson's Social Welfare Function

An economic tool that measures the economic welfare of a given society after considering all relevant economic factors is called the **social welfare function**. There are a number of possible standards for measuring the social welfare of an economy, including financial, social, and political elements. First introduced by the economist **Abram Bergson** in the 1930s, social welfare was posited to be the aggregate level of want-satisfying attainment by all individuals in a society. In a sense, social welfare reflects the values and goals of a society. In the United States, for example, a social and economic goal is to make retired and older citizens who cannot work economically better off. To achieve this social and economic objective, the government has introduced transfer payment programs over the years, primarily through social security. Another objective is to provide those unable to work with sufficient income to be economically viable. Unemployment and disability transfer payments by state and federal governments seek to attain this.

Lorenz Curve

One of the most useful indicators of equality and inequality in income distribution in an economy is the **Lorenz curve**. Developed in the early 20th century by **Max Lorenz**, it paints a graphical representation of the **distribution of income** in a society. The Lorenz curve first posits a state of perfect income equality and compares actual income distribution with the ideal. Another use of the Lorenz curve is to plot the patterns of asset distribution in an economy. The Lorenz curve can indicate what percentage of total income certain economic individuals or households hold. This is done by creating a graph of the curve, with each point measuring relative income. For example, we may learn that 70% of the total income of an economy is held by 30% of the households. The Lorenz curve provides a schedule that charts these ratios. The Lorenz curve and other such relative indicators of income distribution are sometimes used in welfare economics to measure the equality of the economic system. Many social programs are based on these analyses.

Externality in Economic Decisions

When an economic decision made by a person who has no economic gain or loss at stake results in a significant impact on others, it is said to be an **externality**. This occurs when the decision-maker is in a neutral position regarding any gains and losses from the decision. The catalyst for the decision makes economic choices that affect others with no risk. Governments often make such decisions that have an important impact on others but not on the individual who makes the choice. Examples of externalities would be the permission to drill for oil on a nature preserve. The decision may be made in Washington by a government official who has no financial interest in petroleum and does not live near the natural habitat. Yet the decision will have far-reaching effects on a large group of suppliers and consumers. Externalities may usually be traced back to a demand and supply situation. An increased need for oil may have determined the decision for oil exploration in a natural habitat.

Free Goods

In economic analysis, a free good is used rather loosely to designate a good or service that is abundant. This means such goods are available to everyone at little or no cost to the economy. Examples of **free goods** include natural resources owned by the public, water, and air. Some free goods are so easily available that everyone can have as much as they want under ordinary circumstances. Other free goods may be the result of cooperation between economic entities, including governments, to yield an excess of a good for the general welfare. Some free goods are intangible. Examples would include the skies used by airlines, the oceans used to fish and dredge for assets, and ideas or inventions that fall into the public domain. A modern economic intangible is the creation of internet technology, which is a complex combination of ideas, cutting-edge technology, and public access. No one owns the internet, yet is used for a myriad of economic (and personal) purposes.

Tragedy of the Commons

In the constant competition for resources between components of an economy, there arises a phenomenon called "**the tragedy of the commons**." This controversy begs the question as to the ownership of natural resources such as the seas and atmosphere. Can individuals claim as their own the vast resources of the planet, or do they belong to everyone? Should these resources be used for individual gain, or to promote the general welfare? These are the questions raised by the tragedy of the commons, a term coined by **Garrett Hardin**. The concept has been expanded in contemporary economics to describe perceived selfish behavior in all living things. The drive for survival and dominance in nature as well as economics provides many examples of the primacy of **self-interest**. From this self-interest and its results, the **common good** often suffers because of individual actions. This is the larger meaning of the tragedy of the commons.

Modern Examples

Contemporary examples of the tragedy of the commons are evident in all aspects of society. Pollution in all its forms, including air pollution and water pollution, are prime examples of the tragedy of the commons. The irresponsible consumption of logging in forests, depletion of the ocean's resources by over-harvesting and pollution, the indiscriminate littering and graffiti common in cities, and traffic congestion (causing additional pollution and lowered quality of life) are all part of the tragedy of the commons. The less obvious but still destructive examples are noise pollution, legalized gambling, and the seamier sides of the internet, including pornography and massive spamming. These all have negative impacts on the quality of life because of the selfish action of special groups and interests. Whenever there is a degrading of the general welfare in any manner by a small percentage of the population, the tragedy of the commons is seen.

Tragedy of the Anticommons

When there is a collective or individual activity that results in an **under-use** of a scarce resource, this is the **tragedy of the anticommons**. This is contrasted with the tragedy of the commons, which is an overuse or misuse of a scarce resource, which negatively affects the general welfare. If a resource is ignored or underutilized by large numbers of individuals, a different type of waste occurs. This situation is common when a large segment of the economic society is excluded by some means from access to the resource. Common contemporary examples are found in biomedical and pharmacological research, where patents prevent the cooperative development of therapeutic drugs and technology. Property rights are often cited as an example of tragedy of the anticommons, as they exclude a large number of individuals from fully participating in the economic system. When a large part of society is denied access to a fundamental economic activity, that activity may be said to be under-used because the resource is available only to a relative few.

Efficient Market Theory

The mechanisms and activity of capital markets are explained by **efficient market theory**. Using the price of an equity as an example, the price of a stock or bond is a result of all known information and news about the equity and market. This total information results in a rational estimation of the true intrinsic value of the equity. Such a price will have accounted for all positive and negative information of the equity. The price may be said to be **discounted** or **adjusted** for all known information. Should anyone have special access to such information, they are in a position of competitive advantage relative to the equity. This theory makes certain assumptions about the market. These include a large market with many individuals trading for the equity, the presence of perfect information about the stock and market, and free and equal access to all information. Market news is assumed to rise randomly and be available to all at the same time. Efficient market theory is rarely seen in the real world, because the necessary conditions for such a condition to exist almost never occur.

Financial Economics

The branch of economics that deals with business finance, including financing individual firms and corporations, is called **financial economics**. This field also encompasses the financial markets, commodity exchanges, and money markets. Financial economics is governed by several basic principles:

- **Risk or uncertainty** - the gain or loss of monetary assets is not presently known, but will be determined in the future by economic determinants.
- **The element of time** - the monetary gain or loss changes over time.
- **Economic options** - any party to an economic exchange is free to make a decision that will affect future results.
- **Economic information** - economic information can alter future economic activity, result in monetary gains and losses, and change the dynamics of the participants.

Financial economics considers the determinants of prices of financial assets, alternatives for business financing, and personal business decisions that result in reaching economic objectives.

Time Value of Money

A basic precept of business finance is the **time value of money**. Known also as the discounted present value of money, this principle is crucial in decision-making in business finance. Stated simply, the time value of money means an individual would rather have his or her money now than in the future. If the possession of the money is deferred, a price is paid for the delay. This price reflects the time value of money. For example, if $10 today will accrue to $12 in one year, the time value of money for that period is $2. The time value of money is about **future risk**. The value of money today might be worth more or less in the future, depending on inflation or deflation. An investor or lender (or borrower) gives up a certain value today for an uncertain value sometime in the future. Astute individuals will evaluate economic conditions with a view toward predicting the future value of money and base their economic decisions on that projection.

Business Finance

Corporate or managerial finance is the process of acquiring and using funds for business operations. This requires an assessment of potential risk and opportunity for the utilization of monies. Decisions regarding the capital structure of a firm, either by equity financing or the issuing of bonds, must be made. The monies necessary for operations, or working capital, may be provided by income from operations or by a line of credit from a lending institution. Firms may choose to issue bonds to finance operations. The company may then sell the bonds, which carry an interest rate, to investors. These bonds may be traded on the open market, and the price will fluctuate with interest rates. Financial managers of companies may choose to use profits to invest in an array of possible investments, each positioned for a different strategy. The financial function of businesses is critical for their success, both in the shortterm and over a long period. Strategies vary according to the overall position of the firm, its industry goals, and the financial health of the firm.

Risk

Risk is the possible negative effect a business activity or decision carries. **Risk assessment** includes both the probability of a negative event and the assessment of the impact of the potential event. Risk varies from industry to industry and can be applied to a variety of business (or individual) decisions. Risks are an inevitable part of business, and the object of a firm is to minimize risk and maximize return. **Business risks** include marketing decisions, financial choices, production and product delivery systems, and a myriad of other business functions. **Financial risks** are considered to be excellent testing grounds for other business decisions. Current thinking in risk appraisal involves predicting the level of exposure and vulnerability if the potential risk is realized. Managers ask themselves what results they would be willing to live with should the risk become an event. This assessment includes a multitude of factors that must be considered, depending on the nature and possible impact of the risk in question.

General Equilibrium Theory

General equilibrium theory provides a picture of the entire economy, beginning with individuals and their markets. An important part of microeconomics, it models an infinite number of markets for goods and services, beginning with the most basic units in the economy. In this manner, it portrays the entire economy as a sum of all its individual units. It differs from macroeconomics, which begins its analysis of the economy using aggregate numbers. **Modern general equilibrium theory** is a highly sophisticated tool and requires the use of computer technology to generate its models. The vast numbers of individuals and markets included in such an analysis would not have been possible until the widespread use of computers in economic analysis. Generating economic aggregates from individual transactions allows economists to build a model of the economy with a degree of accuracy. It answers the question of how macroeconomics obtains its data. A relatively new tool of economists, the general equilibrium theory promises both comprehensive and accurate raw material with which to build a model of the entire economy.

Neoclassical Economics in Depth

Neoclassical economics is founded on certain assumptions about economic activities. Based on the theories of supply and demand, it assumes all economic units are making rational decisions. Each unit will attempt to maximize their gain or individual economic satisfaction through these decisions, which are based on the economic information available to them. **Neoclassical economics** is, to a large degree, what we call **mainstream economic theory**. Critics of neoclassical economics have been effective in showing obvious flaws in many of the assumptions of the school. These criticisms have often evolved into new schools of economic thought, seeking to find a more realistic way of understanding economic decisions and their results. The very definition of what constitutes neoclassical economics is an area of debate, as neoclassical economists have a wide variety of approaches and analyses for most economic problems. The areas of disagreement from within neoclassical economics and from those who challenge the basic premises of the field have caused a degree of confusion in economic study. It is safe to say that neoclassical economics is in a state of relative flux as new and revised thinking is brought to economic analysis.

Austrian School of Economics and Carl Menger

The 20th century saw the birth of the **Austrian school of economics**, a hybrid school that stands outside the traditional schools of mainstream economic theory. Perhaps the most important proponent of the Austrian school is **Carl Menger**, who, with his associates and colleagues, pioneered the economic theory upon which the Austrian school was founded. **Anti-Keynesian** in approach, the Austrian school has rejected the bioeconomic model of imposing the principles of life sciences to the subject of economics. Employing a logical and intuitive set of tools collectively called **praxeology**, the Austrian school takes a more formal approach to economic theory. The success of the Austrian school has been influential by focusing on the generative stage of economic productivity. It has successfully challenged the behavioral basis of economic theory, in favor of more traditional formal aspects of cause and effect in economic theory. Groups or political associations that profess a libertarian or liberal philosophy view the Austrian school favorably and share many of their social and political goals.

Behavioral Economics

Behavioral economics draws heavily from a number of social sciences and related fields to attempt to understand the behaviors and emotional components of economic activities. Working with the traditional economic framework of allocation of scarce resources, supply, demand, and pricing policy, **behavioral economics** inquires of the reasoning and motivation for economic choices. Behavioral economists study the rational behavior of economic entities and attempt to predict results based on these rational decisions. Behavioral economics posits "**heuristics**," that decision making is often intuitive or behavioral rather than strictly rational. It believes that the way an economic choice is presented to a firm or individual will determine its ultimate decision. Behavioral economics also tackles the phenomena of market inefficiencies, explaining why the behavior of markets often defy logical and expected outcomes.

Criticisms

Opponents of **behavioral economics** often base their arguments on the rational activities of an economy and its units. They contend that the behaviorists ignore market realities, particularly the ability of economic units to learn, modify their choices, and improve their opportunities for success. They feel these factors will move all players in the market toward rational decision-making, upon which neoclassical economics is built. They also claim that cognitive theories do not reflect general economic activity but rather focus on a narrow area of decision-making. Thus, decision-making using a cognitive model cannot be validly imposed on economic decisions. Behavioral economics relies upon surveys and questionnaires to obtain data on economic choices. Critics feel these tools are often poorly constructed and fail to consider that revealed preferences are more accurate in predicting economic behavior than responses from surveys. Bias and subjectivity are sometimes incorporated into the research tools of behavioral economics, making them suspect.

Ecological Economics

The increasing importance of ecology in the last half of the 20th century gave rise to the innovative field of **ecological economics**. This branch of economics concerns itself with the relationships between economics and extant ecosystems in the biosphere. It has common elements with the "green" movement and incorporates human development theory into its approach to economics. The major goal of ecological economics is to protect and preserve resources through **sustainable development** of those resources. Sustainable development means that the resource in question will not be exploited and destroyed by irresponsible economic activity. Ecological economics positions itself as a subdivision of ecology, maintaining that economics is inherent in the interaction of ecosystems in the biosphere. It tends to place an increased importance on the use and misuse of natural resources, which are seen to be the most important of the factors of production.

Profit

The word *profit* is derived from the Latin word *proficere*, whichmeans "to go forward or advance." In an economic sense, **profit** is the gain made from an economic transaction made by a business or individual. Profit may be defined in a multitude of ways, depending on the economic system and the method of accounting within that system. In **investment transactions**, profit is understood to be the return over time of an input of land, labor, and capital. In **business concerns**, this is usually expressed as a rate of return for the assets utilized. Most business concerns measure profit as the difference between revenue received and costs. Economists broaden this definition to include the return from an economic action when the opportunity costs of all other possible choices are considered. The drive for businesses to maximize profits is considered a stimulus to economic activity. It provides motivation and actual rewards for astute economic decisions.

Business Competition

Competition is the driving force that is the lifeblood of capitalism. It tends to motivate innovations and promotes efficient use of resources and profits. Microeconomic theory holds that **competition** is the most important factor in determining resource allocation. Competition forces companies to develop new products and improve existing ones. It spurs technology, refines production capability, and thus provides consumers with an abundance of superior products and services. Competition tends to stabilize prices and insures no one major supplier can dominate an industry. Competition may find two products competing head-to-head in direct competition. Sometimes, firms develop similar products that may be used instead of existing ones, an example of **substitute competition**. Most competition is seen in pricing, production costs, product mixes, marketing, channels of distribution, and consumer satisfaction. These elements fall under the umbrella of **budget competition**.

Wage Determination

The value of **real wages** can only be accurately measured when the productivity of labor is known. Real wages rise when increased levels of technology and per capita investment in labor occurs. The totality of all firms' demand for labor is called the **total market demand for labor**. The market supply of labor depends on the population, level of skill required, prevalent economic condition, and effective wage rate. When the demand and supply curves for labor intersect, the **competitive equilibrium wage rate** is determined. Firms will continue to hire labor until the marginal revenue product of labor, or its demand for labor, reaches the wage rate. **Labor unions** can distort the supply and demand for labor, and thus the wage determination, by increasing productivity, reducing the labor force with excessive union dues, and bargaining with businesses and threatening strikes. All of these activities enter into the determination of wages.

Rent and Interest

Land and other natural resources are limited in supply and thus scarce in economic terms. The price of using land and associated resources is called **rent**. Pricing rent differs from other factors of production, as the total amount of land is fixed. The market demand and price of rent paid do not change the amount of land available for use. **Interest** may be expressed as the price of using money over a period of time, usually expressed in a percentage ratio. Interest rates vary, often to a large degree, depending on the competitive environment, the amount of risk in the loan, the length of the loan, and associated administrative costs involved with the loan. Demand for funds comes from individuals, businesses, and governments. The supply of money available for loan is the accrued aggregate savings of businesses and individuals. This supply is largely determined by the money supply available, which in turn is affected by the monetary policies of the government.

Theory of Games and Economic Behavior, Handbook of Econometrics, and The Handbook of Experimental Economics.

1. *Theory of Games and Economic Behavior* - John Von Neumann and Oskar Morgenstern

Description: A book by the mathematician John von Neumann and economist Oskar Morgenstern. It contains a mathematical theory of economic and social organization, based on a theory of games of strategy. This is now a classic work, upon which modern-day game theory is based.

2. *Handbook of Econometrics* - Zvi Griliches and M. D. Intriligator (eds.)

Description: a five-volume work that is the definitive study of econometrics.

3. *The Handbook of Experimental Economics* – J. H. Kagel and A. E. Roth (eds.)

Description: the most influential experimental economics handbook.

Some of the most important new theories and concepts in microeconomics are published in academic journals such as the *Journal of Econometrics*, *Journal of the American Statistical Society*, and the *Journal of Monetary Economics*. A number of professional business journals offer excellent material.

Poverty Line

The term *poverty line* is commonly used in assessing the success or failure of an economic system. A level of income that fails to reach the minimum for people to purchase the necessities of life is the **poverty line**. Individuals or households falling below this line are unable to provide for themselves and have zero disposable income. Of course, a key consideration is where to draw the poverty line on the economic scale. Because of different prices, costs of living, and varied wage scales, poverty lines are different for each country. When comparing poverty lines between countries, the accepted standard is the **purchasing power exchange rate**. This reveals the relative ability between countries to buy, say, a loaf of bread. Poverty exists to some degree in almost all economic systems. The line is an excellent tool to measure the number and percent of those living in poverty and may form the basis of remedial social programs.

Large Market Share and Public and Government Opposition

As companies grow, it becomes more difficult to increase **market share** regularly. They may diversify into related industries but at the cost of some economies of scope and scale. If a firm grows too large and becomes too successful, it may attract negative publicity and even the attention of the government's **regulatory agencies**. Microsoft is an example of a firm whose dominance attracted unwelcome intervention from external sources. Walmart is another successful corporation that has faced negative publicity and public scrutiny. While these are extreme examples, they occur with some frequency in the corporate world. Larger companies tend to be those who have been in business for a long time and are set on older policies that may not apply to current business conditions. They incur additional fixed costs from pension funds, company benefits, and time lost through sickness. They often control larger portions of the market, making percentage growth more difficult each year. Labor costs may include meeting union demands and the possibility of strikes or work stoppages.

Suggested Retail Price and MSRP

Manufacturers will often make a recommendation as to the **retail price** of a product. This is usually an effort to ensure that the product is sold at a similar price in various locations. Retailers take different approaches to these suggested prices. Some will adhere to the suggested price, while others will discount the price and feature the reduced price as a promotion. Retailers may use their size and/or market position to price goods significantly cheaper than more poorly positioned retailers. An example of this is the price comparisons on almost all unregulated goods between discount houses, convenience stores, and normal retail outlets. Often, prices are set based on the wholesale prices charged to the retailers by suppliers.

Fair trade laws were enacted to protect small retailers from unfair competition from discount houses and chain retail operations. These laws were deemed to be illegal, as they restrained free trade. Manufacturers responded with the **Manufacturers Suggested Retail Price (MSRP)**, which only provides guidelines for retailers. Usually, the MSRP is heavily discounted in order to suggest a product is an excellent bargain at that price.

Revealed Preference Theory

Predicting the buying patterns by consumers can be measured by the **revealed preference theory**, first articulated by **Paul Samuelson**, author of a best-selling economics textbook and a leading figure in contemporary economics. Samuelson postulated that past buying habits could be used to analyze and predict future consumer activity. Samuelson posited that if a consumer purchases a certain brand of ice cream, he or she will continue to do so until something changes his or her mind. Such a change might involve ice cream prices, better-quality ice cream available from a competitor, discontinuation of a favorite flavor or brand, or a host of other conscious and unconscious variables. The consumer may decide to lose weight and give up ice cream as a staple of his or her diet. It can readily be seen that determining these consumer preferences is difficult since it is impossible to know all the factors involved in consumer decisions. Even so, revealed preference theory provides a base from which economists can study purchasing habits of individuals.

Indifference Curves

Indifference curves are another example of a microeconomic tool that measures consumer activity. **Indifference curves** graphically display points on a spectrum where consumers are indifferent to a choice between two products. An indifference curve showing an individual's preference for, say, shirts, might indicate that the desire for a polo shirt and a turtleneck shirt was identical. Thus, both the polo and turtleneck shirts would all be located on the same point of the indifference curve. Indifference curves were introduced as microeconomic tools by economists early in the 20th century. It stemmed from the understanding that consumer satisfaction could be accurately measured. This was called "**cardinal utility**." The new concept uses the principle of "**ordinal utility**," relying on individual economic decisions that could be objectively observed, analyzed, contrasted, and compared, to become the basis for future predictions. From this graphical presentation of data, economists hope to better understand past consumption patterns and future buying activity.

Utility

Utility is a technical economic term that seeks to measure the want-satisfying power of goods and services purchased by consumers. Everyone rationally attempts to increase their **utility**, that is to say, increase their satisfaction gained by economic choices. All goods and services may be measured on an economic scale that rates the utility of that product. Consumer choices (and all microeconomic choices) are made to increase overall utility for that entity. Some goods and services have **increasing utility**, the ability to better satisfy the individual's needs. Others have **decreasing utility**, less effective as want-satisfying products. Utility is combined with other economic tools such as indifference curves to attempt to measure and predict consumer behavior. Utility is also an important feature of welfare economics, where it is used to attempt to create the most satisfaction for the most people in an economy. The concept of utility as an economic tool was pioneered by Jeremy Bentham in the 17th century as an aspect of political economy.

Cardinal and Ordinal Utility

Economists have striven for centuries to improve the economic position of society as a whole. This goal spurred economists to attempt to **measure utility** in a meaningful way in order to maximize it for society. If utility could be measured for an individual, it was postulated that the aggregate utility for society could also be measured. This was called **cardinal utility**. The problem with attempting to measure cardinal utility is the difficulty of measuring utility without an objective means of analyzing the information. Each individual has a different set of needs and wants, and comparing a product's utility between diverse groups is impossible. Cardinal utility was abandoned as a useful tool in economics and replaced by the concept of ordinal utility. **Ordinal utility** applied the scientific method to utility by observing patterns of prior economic behavior, comparing economic variables, and postulating predictions of future activity. This has proved to be a more valuable approach in economic analysis.

INCOME

Income is the compensation received by economic units during the normal activities of business. This includes monies received from multiple sources, including employers, investments, and gifts. In the business world, **gross income** is the amount a company earns before expenses. **Net income** is the money the company has earned after paying the costs of doing business. A company's revenue flow starts with monies received from goods and services sold to consumers. From this amount must be subtracted all monies spent in the operations of the business. This includes employee salaries, costs of production, fixed and variable costs of doing business, and any intangible costs. The resulting figure is the firm's **income** (or loss). If a profit is made, this may be paid as additional compensation to owners, appropriate tax levies, or reinvested to improve the company's position in some respect. Publicly held corporations may choose to pay their stockholders a dividend.

PER CAPITA INCOME AND PERSONAL INCOME

The calculation of per capita income is made by taking the total of all monies earned by residents of a particular area divided by the number of inhabitants of the region. Note that **per capita income** is based on where the individuals live, rather than where they physically work. The aggregate of all monies, including passive income, is called **total personal income**. This figure includes all earnings paid to individuals, transfer payments (social security for example), and investment income from all sources. The relative economic health of a particular area can be measured in part by per capita income and total personal income. **Passive income** is also accounted for in total personal income. These are monies derived from rents, private portfolios of stocks and bonds, earned interest from any source, and various payments from pension funds and other employee retirement programs. Another class of income is derived from **government transfer payments**. These include various social and disability benefits, as well as compensation for the unemployed.

INFORMATION ASYMMETRY

In any economic transaction, a party with superior information commands a great advantage. When this is the case, **information asymmetry** is said to exist. An example would be the seller of a home knowing certain structural weaknesses that the buyer does not know. Frequently, **sellers** have more information because they are privy to details about their own property. Occasionally, **buyers** may have the advantage in knowledge. Information asymmetry allows dishonest sellers to sell inferior or substandard products to buyers who are unaware of the information. In a market with broad information asymmetry, the value of all products in the market, good and bad, may decline because of the lack of trust by buyers. If the situation is too commonplace, the market will fail. Knowledgeable consumers will no longer be willing to participate in such an unfair market.

ECONOMIES OF AGGLOMERATION

There are important benefits to be gained when companies follow a strategy of locating themselves physically close to each other. This strategy and the benefits it yields are called **economies of agglomeration**. Most commonly used in urban areas where multiple similar firms operate, economies of agglomeration is useful in various ways. It provides for a network effect valuable in efficiency in receiving raw materials, drawing from experienced labor pools, and creating competitive advantages in many ways. This is true whether the companies grouped together are complementary or competitive. Both suppliers of raw materials and potential buyers will find it more convenient to work with companies that are physically near each other. Some areas, such as

Silicone Valley, are associated with particular industries. **Diseconomies of agglomeration** also exist when firms group close together. Buyers may shop competitively more easily in a small geographic area. Numerous plants and manufacturing operations can degrade the quality of life in an area. A balance of these factors usually occurs in most modern urban areas.

INCOME INEQUALITY DISTRIBUTION MEASUREMENT

The measurement of income distribution in an economy is done by a set of analytical tools collectively called **income distribution metrics**. The overall purpose of this analysis is to identify patterns of wealth in a society and determine the fairness or inequality of the economy. One set of techniques sets a standard for income and then determines the number of individuals who fall below that line. This approach is most effective in measuring the degree of poverty in a given economy. Examples of these tools in the United States include the poverty line and the number of people living below it. Another group of tools compares income levels between groups and individuals in order to determine how income is distributed in a society and locate patterns of inequality. There are a number of these types of analytical techniques, with the relative poverty line and the Lorenz curve being the best known.

POVERTY LINES

The development of poverty lines is an issue each economy faces as it develops social and economic policy. Some countries use a base figure and adjust it for inflation and deflation. The criteria used to determine the fixed figure can vary between countries to a large degree. Comparing **poverty lines** among countries is a complex and sometimes frustrating problem, as prices, wages, and standards fluctuate over time. For example, the European Common Market first computes the median household income and then arbitrarily sets the poverty line at 60% of that figure. In the United States, the poverty line is based on a Social Security system that makes certain arbitrary levels of income as poverty levels. The government then uses transfer payments to ensure a minimum income to all households based on a tangle of federal, state, and local regulations. While this is admirable from a social point of view, it remains vague and arbitrary from an economic perspective.

ABSOLUTE POVERTY

Absolute levels of poverty exist only in economic theory. It is not economically possible to project a **universal poverty line** for all individuals in the world. This imaginary poverty line cannot fluctuate even if income distribution changes. The theoretical basis for this universal poverty line is that there is a minimum amount of goods necessary to survive and that that amount does not vary worldwide. To accurately compute such a figure, the total of all consumption must be known and accounted for. This is not possible from a practical point of view. **Absolute poverty** will decline when everyone's income in an economy rises, even if the distribution of wealth does not change. An absolute poverty rate may decline, regardless of whether inequality is remedied, as long as the neediest obtain some increase in income. From this brief analysis, it can be seen that an absolute poverty line is meaningless in and of itself. Unless a comparison of income levels within the same economy is measured, there is never a guarantee of accurate and meaningful poverty lines.

RELATIVE POVERTY

Only when a poverty line is fixed in relationship to other economic information does it have validity in the real world. A poverty line must be **relative** to some other economic indicator. For example, median income may be a relative standard with which to measure poverty. One could then define poverty as a certain percentage of income below the median income. In such a case, the general increase in income in a society may increase, but the poverty line will remain the same. Poverty can be thought of as inequality in income, rather than a specific level of income. An evening of income distribution will cause relative poverty to fall. Welfare economists sometimes prefer the term *inequality* to *relative poverty*. The subjective nature of defining poverty is apparent. For example, a level of income that more than takes care of necessities may still be relatively low for the economy as a whole. The arbitrary assignment of a poverty level relative to other economic measurements is by definition subjective.

Social Costs

Every economic decision has a **social cost** closely linked to it. The technical definition of the social costs of an economic action is the aggregate cost of that activity to society as a whole, as well as any costs incurred by the unit or agency making the decision. **Negative externality** is a situation that takes place when the social cost to society is greater than the cost to the decision-maker. The classic example of negative externality is manufacturing pollution. This has a huge social (and economic) cost that is seldom paid for directly by the firm causing the pollution. When the costs are greater to the private sector than to society, a **positive externality** is in effect. Social costs are a major topic and economic measurement in welfare economics. Activists measure social costs and employ them in their arguments for social, political, and economic policy.

Purposes and Effects of Taxation

Any assessment or charge to an individual economic unit by a government or quasi-government may be termed a **tax**. Some taxes are **direct**, such as a sales tax on goods and services sold. Other taxes may be **indirect**, property taxes being a prime example. Taxation has a long history dating back to biblical times. It is often mentioned in the Old and New Testaments. Earlier economic systems received "taxes" as goods and services rendered to a ruling authority. In contemporary economics, we usually think of taxes in terms of legal currency. Taxes have caused revolutions ("No taxation without representation"), have overturned governments, and have become a social and political issue of controversy and debate. Who should pay taxes, how much should be paid, and the use of tax revenue are all critical issues in the fabric of society. The branch of formal economics most concerned with taxes is public finance.

Taxation

Nations, states, and local governments use taxes to finance their operations and for special purposes. **Tax revenues** are typically used for public utilities, promoting of public safety and defense, reinvesting in capital improvement and replacement projects for the public, general operating expenses of the state, and funding public and welfare services. Other uses for tax revenues include social benefits for retired and disabled citizens, public transportation systems, compensation for those unable to work, educational uses, public health and healthcare systems, and waste removal operations. Governments also use taxes to stimulate or contract the economy, alter resource allocations in the economic system, ensure an equitable tax burden on all citizens, and change patterns of income distribution for members of society. Taxation and its revenues have become an important proactive tool for economists attempting to fine-tune macroeconomic activities.

Tax Rates

Tax rates are a percentage figure levied on the tax base to raise revenues. When the tax base is a good, service, or property, the tax is called an **ad valorem tax**. Examples of ad valorem taxes are common, including most property and sales taxes. Value-added taxes, common in Western Europe, add a "hidden" tax to all goods and services (with a few exceptions), computed on the added value at each stage of the manufacturing process. An **excise tax** is a tax levied on a tax base of a determined figure. Excess profit taxes are an example of an excise tax. Tax rates may be either marginal rates or average rates. To compute the **average tax rate**, the total tax revenue is compared to the total tax base as a ratio. **Marginal tax rates** are those imposed on the next unit of currency earned. For example, in a progressive income taxation system, the marginal tax rate will differ from person to person, depending on their income. **Tax brackets** are typically the framework for determining marginal rates of taxes at various income levels.

Flat, Progressive, and Regressive Taxation

A flat tax is one in which the same tax rate applies to all levels of income. For example, a country may have an income tax of 40% on every taxpayer's income, regardless of the level. Someone earning $10,000 a year would pay 40% of that figure. Another individual earning $100,000 a year would pay the same tax rate, 40%, but the dollar amount would differ dramatically. **Regressive tax systems** have a reduced schedule of tax rates as income rises. Thus, someone making $10,000 a year would pay a higher tax rate than someone making $100,000 a year. **Progressive income tax systems**, on the other hand, tax higher levels of income more than lower levels. Progressive tax systems are thought to be the most fair, as they place the largest tax burden on those with the most income. People are seldom happy with any system of taxation, and the entire issue has become a political one, with almost all people calling for tax reform of one type or another.

Income Tax

Most income tax systems in modern economies are **progressive** in that they increase the tax rate as income rises. Progressive tax systems are favored by those who feel the brunt of taxation should be on those who can more easily afford it. Conservative economists (and politicians) argue that this form of taxation is punishing the economically successful and is a deterrent to economic growth. The nature of tax collection and the private information required to administer the system angers some who feel the government is increasingly intrusive in their lives. The nature of tax collection was revolutionized by the concept of **withholding** taxes directly from an individual's paycheck. This serves to aid tax compliance, as the taxes are automatically collected each pay period. Psychologically, it seems less burdensome to the taxpayer who never actually has the money. People have come to accept their salaries as being "take home pay," the actual disposable income available to them after taxes are withheld.

Capital Gains and Corporation Taxes

Capital gains taxes may be levied whenever a major capital asset is sold. **Capital gains taxes** may be applied as a regular tax when the capital gain is called income. In certain circumstances, special tax rates apply to capital gains, and a part of the gain is exempt from taxation. **Corporations** and affluent individuals are the beneficiaries of capital gains tax schedules. Tax rules, statutes, and tax codes provide a number of tax shelters for corporations. Tax "loopholes" are exploited by corporate tax attorneys and accountants to minimize the tax burden of corporations. Income earned by corporations also may benefit from special tax rates. Depreciation of major assets and deductions for major assets provide favorable tax breaks for corporations. Corporations may exempt or defer taxes from income flow by using these special considerations. **Corporate taxes** are often the targets of criticism from social and economic activists who feel they are granted special privileges not available to individuals.

Property Taxes, Inheritance Tax, and Personal Property Tax

Real estate is subject to taxation in the form of a **property tax**. Property taxes may also be levied by governments for personal property such as automobiles. The usual method of determining a property tax is to assess the value of the property on a regular basis and apply the existing tax rate to this base. Property taxes are a prime method of financing education in the United States. Taxes on **estates** and on **inheritances** have both their advocates and critics. Some believe large estates should be taxed, as they are most able to pay. Others argue this discriminates against the wealthy and economically successful individuals. As mentioned above, **personal property taxes** may be levied on many kinds of assets, including vehicles and boats. Critics argue there is no rationale for these taxes and they simply serve to fill government coffers. Auto registration and license fees at least offer a privilege (driving) for their levy.

International Trade and Tariffs

Tariffs are, in effect, a tax on goods imported from other countries. Goods cannot be delivered and sold before a tariff is paid. **Tariffs** have broad implications in international trade and, consequently, in relations between nations. Tariffs may be calculated by the weight of goods, or as a percentage of the value of the item (ad valorem). Sometimes, governments impose tariffs as a purely money-making function, and these are termed **revenue tariffs**. Tariffs are widely used by countries to protect their own exports and to defend their own industries from competition from abroad. Tariffs add to the price of imported goods, affording a price advantage to local products. A protective tariff can be so high as to be prohibitive, so that no imports are economically viable. Tariffs have become both political and economic weapons for competing nations. Tariffs have historically been opposed by "free traders," who believe unfettered trade is the healthiest economic environment and works to the benefit of all countries involved.

Evolutionary Economics in Depth

Evolutionary economics is a new and growing field in heteroeconomics. Modeled on the life sciences, it looks at economic activity as complex, dynamic interactions with elements of scarcity, growth, and the striving for competitive advantages. In a sense, **evolutionary economics** imposes Darwin's theory of evolution on economic conditions to explain both behavior and results. **Survival of the fittest** may be applied to business concerns, with the most adaptable succeeding and those unable to select economic survival capabilities failing and forced to suspend operations. Firms must survive by combining a product mix appropriate for their markets with effective business practices. As conditions change, those businesses that are able to maintain flexibility and measured responses to a changing economic environment will survive, while less responsive firms will fall away. Companies that succeed tend to continue innovative practices that allow them to achieve success. Those who fail to respond to economic change will not survive in the long run.

Agricultural Economics

Agricultural economics reflects a more businesslike approach to economics and is focused on the individual units active in agricultural activities. Courses in **agricultural economics** in colleges and universities tend to emphasize business practices as they relate to agriculture. By definition, this gives agricultural economics a microeconomic flavor. The field of study in agricultural economics relates to the supply of farm commodities and domestic animals. Included in the broader scope of the field are the area of rural development, the economics of production for farm goods, and the business-oriented areas of agribusiness management. Although a specialized field of economics, general economic principles such as risk, resource allocation, markets, competition, and international trade are all an important part of agricultural economics. Specialized topics include food safety, crop protection, farm production methods and techniques, rules and regulations governing agricultural economics, and the critical importance of the field to the well-being of society.

Direct and Indirect Taxation

Direct taxes are defined as those that are imposed and collected directly from the economic units being taxed. For example, income taxes are levied and collected from the individual or business that actually receives monies as income. **Indirect taxes**, by contrast, are collected from a third party who is not the being actually taxed. Value-added taxes are indirect taxes, hidden from the consumer who pays an increased retail or wholesale price that includes the value-added tax. **Statutes** determine for whom the tax is being collected. The individual who ends up paying the tax is another matter. For example, a tax may be placed on alcoholic beverages of all kinds. Only those who choose to consume these products will actually be subject to the tax. Laws of supply and demand in the marketplace will determine the individuals that will pay this tax. If an individual chooses not to buy wine, beer, or liquor, they will be, in effect, exempt from that tax. The more a person consumes the taxed items, the more tax will be paid by that individual.

Chapter Quiz

Ready to see how well you retained what you just read? Scan the QR code to go directly to the chapter quiz interface for this study guide. If you're using a computer, simply visit the online resources page at **mometrix.com/resources719/apmicroeconom** and click the Chapter Quizzes link.

AP Practice Test

Want to take this practice test in an online interactive format?
Check out the online resources page, which includes interactive practice questions and much more: **mometrix.com/resources719/apmicroeconom**

1. Economics is best defined as the study of what?

a. Scarcity
b. Business
c. Trade
d. Supply and demand
e. Efficiency

2. Which of the following statements concerning choice theory are correct?

I. Scarcity forces people, including producers, to make choices
II. Producers make choices and, as a result, face trade-offs
III. Opportunity cost is one way to measure the cost of a choice

a. I only
b. I and II only
c. II and III only
d. I, II, and III
e. III only

3. What measures the impact of choosing one option over another?

a. Supply
b. Elasticity
c. Comparative advantage
d. The Law of Diminishing Marginal Returns
e. Opportunity cost

4. Miguel and Huan both work at a software company. In one hour, Miguel can create one computer graphic or write ten pages of text. In the same hour, Huan can create three computer graphics or write 20 pages of text. Based on this information, it can be said that:

a. Miguel has an absolute advantage in creating computer graphics.
b. Miguel has an absolute advantage in writing pages of text.
c. Miguel has a comparative advantage in creating computer graphics.
d. Miguel has a comparative advantage in writing text.
e. None of the above

5. Ciao Bella Pizza faces this production function when making pizzas:

Pizzas Produced	Total Cost
0	0
1	6
2	12
3	18
4	23
5	28
6	32
7	37
8	43

Which pizza has the lowest marginal cost?

a. First
b. Third
c. Sixth
d. Seventh
e. Eighth

6. Which of the following statements about the production possibilities frontier are correct?

I. Points on the frontier are efficient
II. Points inside the line are efficient
III. Points outside the line are unattainable
IV. The frontier represents all possible production combinations of all goods

a. I and IV
b. II and III
c. I and III
d. II and IV
e. II, III, and IV

7. Which basic questions do all economic systems need to answer?

I. Supply and demand
II. What goods and services will be produced?
III. How goods and services will be produced
IV. To which people will goods be distributed?

a. I only
b. I, II, and III
c. II and IV
d. II, III, and IV
e. IV only

8. What does the distinctive, outwardly bowed shape of the PPF signify?

a. The law of supply and demand
b. The efficiency of the free market system
c. That the two goods do not have constant opportunity costs when producing in different quantities along the PPF.
d. The unequal distribution of wealth within a society
e. The shift in demand to match a corresponding shift in supply

9. According to Adam Smith, what brings about the maximum levels of production of goods and services when faced with limited resources?

a. Opportunity cost
b. Specialization
c. Inelastic demand
d. Monopolistic competition
e. Public subsidies

10. John is considering using $100 dollars to download $100 worth of music, buy $100 worth of video games, or contribute $100 to charity. Which of the following statements correctly defines the opportunity cost of his decision?

a. If John buys music, the opportunity cost is the lost opportunity to buy video games and contribute to charity.
b. If John contributes to charity, there is no opportunity cost.
c. If John contributes to charity, the opportunity cost is the lost opportunity to buy music and video games.
d. If John buys video games, the opportunity cost can be defined as the lost opportunity to buy music or donate to charity.
e. All of the above are correct

11. Thrifty Buy More sells blue baseball hats at $10 a hat in May. The equilibrium price for blue baseball hats increases to $12 in June. Which of the following is a potential explanation for the change?

a. An increase in supply of blue baseball hats
b. A decrease in demand for blue baseball hats
c. Both supply and demand stay the same
d. Government subsides make it less costly to produce blue hats
e. Substitute goods decrease in supply

12. The price of fleece blankets goes up from $10 to $11. At the same time, demand goes down from 1,000 blankets to 800 blankets. Which of the following statements is true?

a. Demand is elastic
b. Demand is inelastic
c. The price elasticity quotient, or E_d, is less than 1
d. The price elasticity quotient, or E_d, is equal to 1
e. Demand is unitary elastic

13. Which of the following statements about price elasticity of supply is not correct?

a. If the percentage change in the quantity supplied is greater than the percentage change in price, the supply is elastic.
b. The supply of a good or service with a short life expectancy, such as fresh grapes, is inelastic.
c. Short-run supply for a factory producing a good through a complicated combination of resources tends to be inelastic.
d. Long-run supply for a factory tends to be more elastic than short-run supply.
e. If E_S is greater than 1, supply is inelastic.

14. Which of the following areas represents consumer surplus?

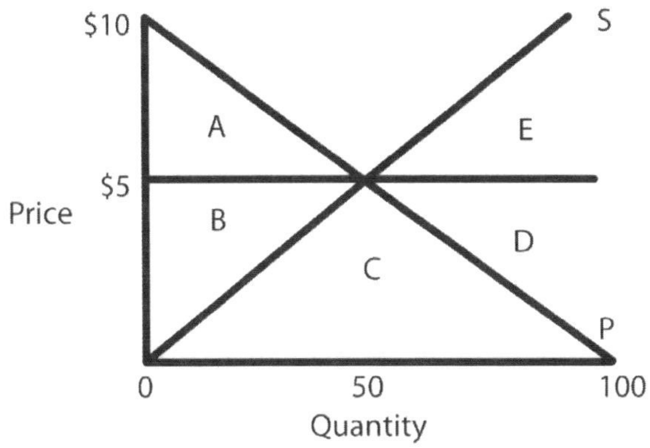

a. A
b. B
c. C
d. D
e. E

15. Which of the following statements is true about producer surplus?

a. It is always the same as consumer surplus
b. It is the part of the demand curve that reaches beyond the equilibrium point
c. A decrease in equilibrium price results in an increase in producer surplus
d. A decrease in equilibrium price results in a decrease in producer surplus
e. An increase in equilibrium price results in a decrease in producer surplus

16. A determinant of demand increases. What follows?

I. The demand curve shifts to the right
II. The equilibrium price increases
III. The equilibrium quantity increases
IV. The supply curve shifts to the left

a. Only I
b. I and II only
c. I, II, and III only
d. I, II, III, and IV
e. None of the above

17. Assume that the equilibrium price for an apartment in Gotham City is $1,000 and the equilibrium quantity 10,000. Now, assume government steps in and creates a price ceiling at $850. Which of the following is likely to occur?

I. Demand will increase
II. Supply will increase
III. A price floor will also be established

a. I only
b. II only
c. III only
d. I and II only
e. II and III only

18. Assume a government places a tax on books. Which area on the map below represents the deadweight loss that results from that tax?

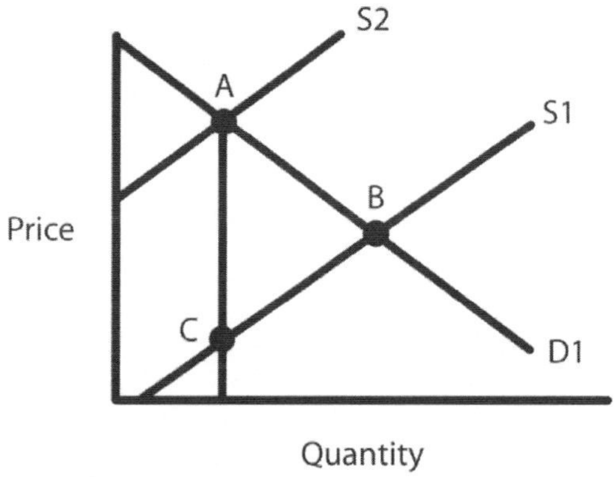

a. The area bounded by points A, B, and C
b. The area left of S2 and right of D1
c. The area between S1 and S2
d. The area left of S2
e. The area right of S1 and left of D1

19. What would you expect if a government price floor is established above the equilibrium price of a good?

a. Shortages of the good
b. Surpluses of the good
c. An increase in demand
d. A decrease in supply
e. Equilibrium price will decrease

20. The price of movies in your town goes down, but the amount that you spend on movies does not change. Which of the following statements is true?

a. Your demand for movies is inelastic
b. Your demand for movies is elastic
c. Your demand for movies is perfectly elastic
d. Your demand for movies is perfectly inelastic
e. None of the above

21. Assume the demand for a company's product is perfectly inelastic. Which of the following is true?

a. An increase in price will lead to a decrease in revenue
b. A decrease in price will lead to an increase in revenue
c. A decrease in price will increase demand
d. An increase in price will decrease demand
e. The demand curve would be vertical

22. Good A and Service B are complements. Which of the following is true?

a. An increase in price for Good A will lead to an increase in demand for Service B
b. A decrease in price for Good A will lead to decreased demand for Service B
c. An increase in demand for Good A will lead to increased revenues for providers of Service B
d. Demand for Good A will not affect demand for Service B
e. An increase in demand for Service B will lead to a surplus of Good A

23. The demand curve for iPhones slopes downward. That means that an increase in the price of iPhones will lead to:

I. More consumers buying other phones
II. More consumers going without phones at all
III. Fewer iPhones available to buy

a. I only
b. II only
c. III only
d. I and/or II only
e. All of the above

24. Ivy got a raise at work and her income has increased. As a result, she buys less Johnson's mascara and more Jackson's mascara. Which statement below best describes this situation?

a. Johnson's mascara and Jackson's mascara are complementary goods
b. Johnson's mascara and Jackson's mascara are normal goods
c. The demand curve for Jackson's mascara is upward sloping
d. The demand curve for Johnson's mascara is upward sloping
e. Johnson's mascara is an inferior good, and Jackson's mascara is a normal good

25. The following table shows the marginal utility, measured in utils, that Kenny receives from purchasing good X and purchasing good Y. Good X costs $5, and good Y costs $10. Kenny has a total of $50 to spend on the two goods each week. If Kenny wants to maximize his total utility, which combination of goods should he buy?

Quantity of X	Marginal Utility of X	Quantity of Y	Marginal Utility of Y
1	8	1	20
2	6	2	12
3	5	3	8
4	4	4	6
5	3	5	4
6	2	6	3
7	2	7	3
8	2	8	2
9	1	9	2
10	1	10	1

a. 0 good X, 5 good Y
b. 2 good X, 4 good Y
c. 4 good X, 3 good Y
d. 6 good X, 2 good Y
e. 10 good X, 0 good Y

26. Jasmine uses her income to maximize her total utility by buying 10 good A's and 5 good B's. Which of the following statements would be true if Jasmine got a raise, increasing her income by 10%?

a. Her buying behavior will not change
b. The marginal utility of good A will increase
c. The marginal utility of good B will increase
d. Her total utility, measured in utils, will increase
e. Her total utility, measured in utils, will decrease

27. Brittany receives a raise at work. After receiving the raise, her purchases of good A increase and her purchases of good B decrease. Which of the above statements are true?

I. Good A is an inferior good
II. Good B is an inferior good
III. Goods A and B are substitute goods
IV. Brittany's total utility through purchases can increase after the raise

a. I and II only
b. II and IV only
c. I and III only
d. II and III only
e. I, II, and III only

28. Randy buys 10 good A's and 10 good B's each week, spending all of his income and maximizing his total utility. His income stays the same, but the price of good B increases. Which of the following is not true?

a. Randy may begin buying good C, a substitute good for good B
b. Randy's total utility will decrease
c. Randy's purchases of good A or good B will decrease
d. Randy's buying behavior will stay the same
e. All of the above

29. Which of the following examples illustrates the law of diminishing marginal utility?

a. When the price of a good increases from $10 to $12, Bob demands less of the good
b. As the supply of a good increases, consumers demand less of the good
c. As Juan buys more units of a single good, he gets less satisfaction from each new purchase
d. As Sally's income decreases, she is forced to reconsider the goods and services she buys
e. As a consumer's income decreases, the total utility he or she derives from that income, measured in utils, also decreases

30. Short-run production is the time period during which _______. Long-run production is the time period during which _______.

a. a company's profits are maximized; a company's profits can be made greater
b. a company's costs are fixed; a company's costs can be decreased
c. a plant's revenue is fixed; a plant's revenue can increase
d. a company's production will not change; a company's production will change
e. a plant's production capacity cannot be changed; a plant's production capacity can be changed

31. What does the data in the following table most directly describe?

Inputs	1	2	3	4
Output	20	50	80	100

a. The Law of Diminishing Marginal Returns
b. Law of Increasing Opportunity Cost
c. Law of Demand
d. Consumer surplus
e. Marginal utility

32. consider the following data showing a company's total output (Q), total fixed costs (TFC), total variable costs (TVC), and total costs (TC).

Total Output	Total Fixed Costs	Total Variable Costs	Total Costs
0	$20	$0	$20
1	$20	$20	$40
2	$20	$38	$58
3	$20	$50	$70
4	$20	$60	$80
5	$20	$70	$90

What is the marginal cost of the 3rd unit of output?

a. $0
b. $12
c. $18
d. $23.33
e. $38

33. Consider the data showing a firm's long-run average total costs.

Units Produced (Q)	0	10	20	30	40	50
Average Total Costs (ATC)	50	40	30	30	40	50

Which of the following are true?

I. As the firm moves from producing 0 units to producing 20 units, it experiences economies of scale
II. As the firm moves from producing 0 units to producing 30 units, it experiences economies of scale
III. The firm experiences constant returns of scale only when producing 20 units

a. I only
b. II only
c. III only
d. I and II only
e. II and III only

34. Assume a company uses two inputs to produce a product. To determine the least-cost, profit-maximizing combination of inputs, what should the company do?

a. Use both inputs to the point where its marginal revenue product is greater than their price
b. Use both inputs to the point where their marginal revenue product is less than their price
c. Use both inputs to the point where their marginal revenue product is equal to their price
d. Use both inputs to the point where their marginal revenue product is highest
e. Use both inputs to the point where their marginal revenue product is lowest

35. Company X is looking at changing the amount of labor used to produce their product. They have determined the following:

Units of Labor Input	Total Product Output	Total Revenue (in $)
1	10	100
2	30	300
3	40	400
4	48	480
5	54	540

Using the data above, the marginal product of 3 units of labor is ______ and the marginal revenue product is ______.

a. 40; 400
b. 10; 100
c. 360; 440
d. 8; 80
e. 13.33; 133.33

36. What would you expect to happen to marginal product as the number of inputs used is increased?

a. It will consistently increase
b. It will consistently decrease
c. It will decrease, stay constant, then increase
d. It will increase, stay constant, then decrease
e. It will stay the same

37. A firm's long run average total cost curve is a curve that connects what?

a. The minimums of the firm's short run average total cost curves
b. The maximums of the firm's short run average total cost curves
c. The minimum of the firm's long run average total costs
d. The maximum of the firm's long run average total costs
e. All of the firm's different short run average total cost curves combined

38. Assume you've invested $1,000,000 to begin a business. At the end of the year, revenues equal $1,200,000. During that same year, you could have worked for $300,000. Which of the following statements is true?

a. Accounting profit equals $200,000
b. Economic profit equals accounting profit
c. Accounting profit equals $300,000
d. Economic profit equals $500,000
e. The economic profit is greater than the accounting profit

39. You've invested $200,000 to start a new business, made revenues of $220,000, and had an opportunity to work for $40,000 during the same time. Which of the following is(are) true?

I. Accounting profit is $20,000
II. Economic loss is (-$20,000)
III. Opportunity cost of starting the new business is $240,000

a. I only
b. II only
c. III only
d. I and II only
e. I, II, and III

40. Assume a business in a perfectly competitive market is operating such that marginal revenue equals marginal cost. Which of the following is true?

a. The firm will increase production
b. The firm will decrease production
c. The firm will continue producing at that quantity
d. The marginal profit of the next item produced will be positive
e. The marginal revenue from the next item produced will be greater than the marginal cost of that item

41. In a perfectly competitive market, which of the following is true of a firm making a short-run loss?

I. Total costs exceed total revenue
II. The firm should continue production as long as revenue is equal to or greater than total variable costs
III. Total revenue exceeds total costs
IV. The firm should shut down if revenue is equal to or greater than total variable costs but less than total costs

a. I and II
b. III and IV
c. I only
d. III only
e. None of the above

42. When should a firm shut down in the short run?

I. If total costs are greater than total revenues
II. If total variable costs are greater than total revenues
III. If total fixed costs are greater than total revenues

a. I only
b. II only
c. III only
d. I and II only
e. I, II, and III

43. A perfectly competitive firm is efficient when:

I. Price = marginal cost
II. Marginal cost = marginal revenue
III. Price = marginal cost = maximum profit

a. I only
b. II only
c. III only
d. II and III only
e. I and II only

44. A profit-maximizing monopolist will produce:

I. At a price higher than the minimum ATC
II. At a price lower than the minimum ATC
III. At an output above the demand of the demand curve and the marginal cost curve
IV. At an output below the intersection of the demand curve and the marginal cost curve

a. I and III only
b. I and IV only
c. II and III only
d. II and IV only
e. I, II, II and IV

45. An unregulated monopoly creates which inefficiencies?

I. Producing at a higher price than a perfectly competitive firm
II. Producing fewer goods than a perfectly competitive firm would
III. Producing where MR = MC

a. I and II only
b. II and III only
c. I and III only
d. I, II, and III
e. None of the above

46. In general, cartels lead to which combination when compared with perfect competition?

a. High prices, increased production
b. Higher prices, lower production
c. Lower prices, higher production
d. Lower prices, lower production
e. Equilibrium of prices and production

47. Which of the following statements is true about an oligopoly?

a. There are no or very few barriers to entry
b. Many firms participate
c. Collusion may be planned or unplanned
d. The demand curve is straight
e. Economies of scale are limited or nonexistent

48. Which of the following is not true of monopolistic competition?

a. There are no great barriers to entry or exit from the market
b. Firms within monopolistic competition benefit from product differentiation
c. Firms within monopolistic competition maximize profit by producing where MR = MC
d. All or most firms within monopolistic competition attain long-run profit
e. Firms in monopolistic competition are efficient

49. Ciao Bella Restaurant has a marginal resource cost of $22 for its last worker and a marginal revenue product of $20 for that same worker. Which of the following is true?

a. Ciao Bella should hire another worker to maximize profits
b. The MRP of the next worker will exceed the MRC
c. Ciao Bella should not hire another worker
d. Producing more will lead to lower marginal costs
e. Producing more will lead to higher profits

50. Which of the market structures is most efficient?

a. Perfect competition
b. Monopolistic competition
c. Oligopoly
d. Monopoly
e. Collusive oligopoly

51. Which of the following statements are true about monopolies?

I. They allocate resources efficiently
II. They maximize profits
III. Price = marginal costs

a. I only
b. II only
c. III only
d. I and II
e. I, II, and III

52. In the long run, firms will exit a monopolistically competitive market when:

a. Profit is maximized
b. Price = marginal cost
c. Price exceeds marginal cost
d. There is an economic profit
e. Price is less than the minimum of the average total costs curve

53. Consider the following short-run data for Bob's Widgets, a perfectly competitive firm:

Total Revenue: $100
Total Costs: $200
Total Fixed Costs: $90
Total Variable Costs: $110

What should Bob's do?

a. Increase production
b. Decrease production but continue to produce
c. Lower fixed costs
d. Shut down
e. Lower prices

54. Firms will attempt to enter a market if the market is:

a. Operating where MR = MC
b. Operating where MC is greater than MR
c. Earning an accounting profit
d. Earning an economic profit
e. Earning a normal profit

55. Consider the following data for a firm's use of labor input:

Input (Labor)	1	2	3	4	5
Product Output	10	30	40	45	47
Total Revenue	$10,000	$30,000	$40,000	$45,000	$47,000

What is the marginal product of labor of the 5th worker hired?

a. 2
b. 23.5
c. 47
d. 2,000
e. 47,000

56. Oil transport is a derived factor of oil sales. What will happen to demand for oil transport if demand for oil increases?

a. It will increase
b. It will stay the same
c. It will decrease
d. None of the above
e. Any of the above—there's not enough information to answer

57. Which of the following is an example of a derived factor?

a. Oil consumption for automobiles
b. Fertilizers for agriculture
c. Educator labor (teachers) for private schools
d. Computer chips for personal computers
e. All of the above

58. What does the Lorenz Curve shown below signify?

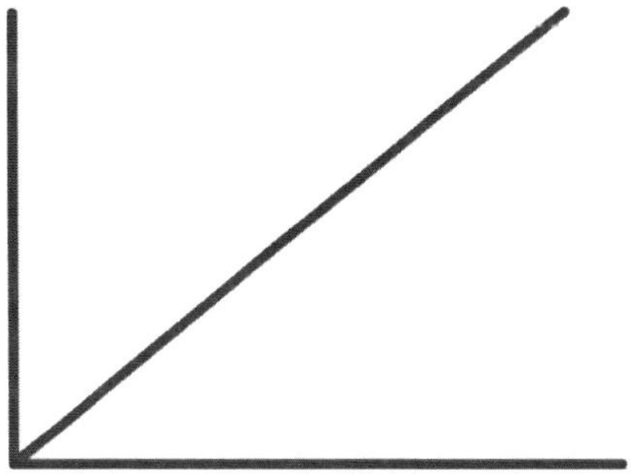

a. Inelastic demand for a product
b. The effect of price caps on supply
c. Perfect equality of income in a population
d. Economic profit in a monopoly
e. Diseconomies of scale in long-run average total costs

59. How will the marginal revenue product curve of a firm in monopolistic industry compare with the marginal revenue product curve of a firm in a perfectly competitive industry?

a. The MRP curve for the monopolist will look the same as the MRP curve for the perfectly competitive industry
b. The MRP curve for the monopolist will slope upward, while the MRP curve for the perfectly competitive firm will slope downward
c. The MRP curve for the monopolist will slope downward, while the MRP curve for the perfectly competitive firm will slope upward
d. The MRP curve for the monopolist will slope downward, while the MRP curve for the perfectly competitive firm will be horizontal
e. The MRP curve for the monopolist will be horizontal, while the MRP curve for the perfectly competitive firm will slope downward

60. Assume the price of a firm's product is $10, the marginal physical product of a potential new worker is 10, and the firm's marginal cost is $110. What will the firm do?

a. Hire the worker
b. Hire the worker and other workers too
c. Not hire the worker
d. Not hire the worker and lay off other workers
e. Plan to shut down in the long run

61. Which of the following is NOT true of a monopsonist or monopsony?

a. A monopsony is a market with just one buyer of a resource input
b. A monopsonist firm will hire additional labor until marginal revenue cost = marginal revenue product
c. A monopsonist faces a downward-sloping supply curve for labor
d. A monopsonist hires less than the efficient amount of labor
e. A monopsonist pays wages under the equilibrium wage rate

62. How will a labor union affect a labor market?

I. Increase supply of labor
II. Decrease supply of labor
III. Increase wage earned by labor
IV. Decrease wage earned by labor

a. I and III only
b. I and IV only
c. II and III only
d. II and IV only
e. I, II, and III

63. In a perfectly competitive labor market, a minimum wage is enforced. The minimum wage is higher than the equilibrium wage rate for the market. Shortly after, the number of potential workers is reduced. Which of the following is true?

I. The supply of workers willing to work at the minimum wage will increase
II. The demand for workers at the minimum wage will decrease
III. Unemployment will increase after the minimum wage is installed
IV. Unemployment will decrease after the supply of labor is reduced

a. I, III, and IV only
b. II and III only
c. I and III only
d. II, III, and IV only
e. I, II, III, and IV

64. Felt and labor are two inputs used to create a particular type of men's hat. If the price of the hats decreases, what else will happen?

I. Demand for felt will increase
II. The price of felt will decrease
III. Demand for hat-making labor will increase
IV. The price of hat-making labor will increase

a. I and III only
b. II and IV only
c. I, II, and III only
d. I, III, and IV only
e. All of the above

65. In the competitive labor market shown, what is the wage rate?

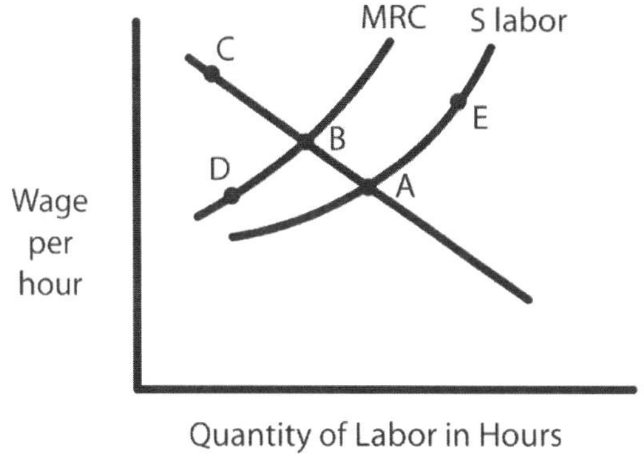

a. A
b. B
c. C
d. D
e. E

66. Assume the US Congress sets a minimum wage rate above the current minimum wage. What is the likely result?

a. More people will be employed
b. Demand for labor will increase
c. Unemployment will decrease
d. Employment will decrease
e. Supply of labor will decrease

67. A company redevelops an old abandoned warehouse, creating an improvement to the neighborhood as a whole. This improvement to the neighborhood is known as what?

a. Private benefit
b. External benefit
c. Social benefit
d. Social cost
e. External cost

68. A company produces a good at a cost of $100. In doing so, it creates a certain level of pollution, unwanted by the neighborhood. The pollution is known as what?

a. Private benefit
b. Opportunity cost
c. Private cost
d. Social cost
e. External cost

69. The impact of a transaction on parties not directly involved in the transaction is known as what?

a. Social cost
b. Social benefit
c. Externality
d. Marginal social cost
e. Marginal social benefit

70. Users of a public good:

a. must pay for the good.
b. cannot be prevented from using the good if they do not pay.
c. do not benefit from the good.
d. do not experience externalities of the good.
e. are prohibited from experiencing the private benefits of the good.

71. How is a public good different than a private good?

I. Users cannot be excluded from using a public good.
II. The use of a public good by one person does not reduce the availability of that good for another person.
III. It is difficult to determine how much a user values a public good.

a. I only
b. II only
c. III only
d. I and II only
e. I, II, and III

72. A new government regulation sets a higher quality standard for televisions. As a result of this regulation:

a. the supply of televisions will increase.
b. the price of televisions will decrease.
c. the price of televisions will increase and supply will decrease.
d. the price of televisions will decrease and demand will increase.
e. None of the above

73. Which of the following statements is not true?

a. If the government imposes a tax on a good, the supply curve will shift to the left
b. If the government imposes a tax on a good, it will result in a deadweight loss
c. If the government imposes a tax on a good with a highly inelastic demand, it will be difficult for producers of the good to shift the cost to consumers
d. If the government imposes a tax on a good, the market price of the good will likely increase
e. If the government imposes a tax on a good, the demand for the good will likely decrease

74. Which of the following statements about public goods is true?

a. The free market excels in producing them
b. When a person uses the good, it prevents others from using the good
c. There is no demand for public goods
d. It is difficult to prevent people from using the good without paying
e. They are equally valued by all people

75. As a result of a news story, citizens in a society develop a new, higher appreciation for a clean environment. Which of the following would result?

I. The marginal cost curve for anti-pollution technologies shifts right
II. The marginal benefit curve for anti-pollution technologies shifts right
III. The supply curve of anti-pollution technologies shifts right

a. I only
b. II only
c. III only
d. I and III only
e. II and III only

76. Proponents of legislating greater societal income equity, support all of the following:

I. Impose a progressive income tax
II. Impose high estate taxes
III. Impose a gift tax

a. I only
b. II only
c. III only
d. I, II, and III
e. II and III only

77. Which of the following terms best describes a sales tax of 8%?

a. Progressive
b. Regressive
c. Progressive-regressive
d. Flat
e. None of the above

78. Which of the following is associated with market failure?

I. When a firm in a non-competitive industry hires labor at a lower wage
II. When the firms in a non-competitive industry create less than the efficient amount of a good or service
III. When production of a good creates negative externalities born by third parties
IV. Public goods

a. I and II only
b. II and III only
c. I and III only
d. I, II, and III only
e. I, II, III, and IV

79. Taxes, subsidies, price ceilings, price floors, taxes, and government regulations are all most commonly used for what purpose?

a. To correct market failure
b. To prevent the formation of trusts
c. To provide public goods
d. To prevent negative externalities
e. To promote an equal distribution of income

80. Which of the following is a role that the US federal government plays in the US economy?

I. Regulation of industries
II. Taxation
III. Provider of safety net for the poor
IV. Provider of public goods

a. I and II only
b. II and III only
c. II and IV only
d. I, II, and III only
e. I, II, III, and IV

Answer Key and Explanations

1. A: Economics is defined as the study of scarcity, the situation in which resources are limited and wants are unlimited.

2. D: It is true that scarcity causes producers (and other people) to make choices. Producers must choose what to produce with limited resources. It is also true that the choices a producer makes when faced with scarcity come with trade-offs. There are advantages and disadvantages to different production decisions. And, finally, calculating the opportunity cost of a choice provides a manner with which to measure the consequence of a choice and compare that against the consequence of other choices.

3. E: The opportunity cost of a producer's choice to produce one good is the loss of the ability to use the same resources to produce another good.

4. D: Miguel has a comparative advantage in writing text because he can create 10 pages of text for an opportunity cost of only 1 graphic for a ratio of 10-1, whereas Huan creates 20 pages of text at an opportunity cost of 3 graphics for a ratio of 20-3 or 10-1.5. Miguel's opportunity cost of 1 graphic per 10 pages of text is less than Huan's opportunity cost of 1.5 graphics per 10 pages of text.

5. C: The marginal cost of each pizza is the cost to make that one additional pizza. In this case, the sixth pizza adds only $4 to the total cost, the lowest of all production levels given.

6. C: The production possibilities frontier, or PPF, represents all the possible production combinations of two goods, not all goods. Points inside the frontier are inefficient because they do not fully utilize all available resources. Points on the frontier are efficient because they maximize the usage of all available resources. Points beyond the frontier are unattainable because they offer combinations of goods that are unavailable due to resource and production limitations.

7. D: An economic system must decide what goods and services are produced, how they are produced, and who gets them. The economic system will not set supply or demand.

8. C: Because the PPF shows all the combinations of goods that can be produced with a given set of resources, it is bowed, signifying that some combinations of the two goods have different opportunity costs.

9. B: A basic element of Adam Smith's thought is that, since economies have access to limited resources with which to produce services, they should specialize in producing those goods and services they can produce most efficiently.

10. D: When making an economic decision, the opportunity cost is the lost opportunity to do the next best alternative. Therefore, options a. and c. are incorrect because they define the opportunity cost as the lost option to do two other things. Option b. is incorrect because giving money to charity has an opportunity cost just like spending money does. Option d. is correct because it says the opportunity cost is either purchasing music or donating to charity --- whichever is preferred would be correct but from the question we do not know which is preferred so "or" is appropriate.

11. E: An increase in the supply of the hats and a decrease in demand would both cause the equilibrium price to decrease, not increase. If both supply and demand stayed the same, the equilibrium price would also stay the same. If government subsidies made it cheaper to produce the hats, the price would go down. If the supply of a substitute good went down, more consumers might be driven to buy the blue hats, causing demand to increase and the equilibrium price to increase with it.

12. A: The change in demand is 20% (1,000 − 800 = 200), and the change in price is 10% ($11 − $10 = $1). Because the change in demand is greater than the change in price, the demand is considered elastic. In this case, the price elasticity quotient is greater than 1.

13. E: It is not true that if E_S is greater than 1, supply is inelastic. In fact, that is the definition of elastic supply. All the other options are true—a. is another way to define elastic supply, b. is true because the supplier has to sell the goods before they perish, c. is true because production processes are generally fixed in the short run, and d. is true because, given time, a producer can change supply.

14. A: Consumer surplus is the area below the demand curve that is above the equilibrium price line, represented by Area A in this graph.

15. D: Producer surplus is the area above the supply curve and below the equilibrium price line. If the equilibrium price decreases, the area between the supply curve (unchanged) and the price line (lowered) will be smaller – which means a decrease in producer surplus.

16. C: I, II, and III are correct. If a determinant of demand increases, demand will increase. That means that the demand curve will shift to the right, causing an increase in both the equilibrium price and the equilibrium quantity. An increase in a determinant of demand will not cause any movement to the supply curve.

17. A: If a price ceiling is established, demand will increase. Supply, however, will decrease. A price floor must be placed at a price higher than the equilibrium price in order for it to have any effect on the market, and the government would not simultaneously institute a price ceiling and a price floor.

18. A: Deadweight loss, which is the reduction in efficiency and the decrease in societal welfare, is represented by the area bounded by point A (the original equilibrium price), point B (the price consumers pay for the good), and point C (the price producers receive for the good).

19. B: If the government establishes a price floor that is higher than the equilibrium price, supply will exceed demand, and there will be a surplus.

20. B: Your demand for movies is elastic because as the price decreased, you went to more movies, as evidenced by the fact that you spent the same amount of money.

21. E: If demand for a firm's product is perfectly inelastic, consumers will buy the same amount no matter the price. Therefore, the demand curve will be a straight line traveling up and down on the graph. A price increase would lead to an increase in revenue, a price decrease would lead to a decrease in revenue, and no price change would affect demand.

22. C: Complementary goods or services are goods for which demand is linked. If demand for a good increases, the demand for the good's complement will also increase. It follows, then, that increased demand for Good A will lead to increased demand for Service B, which in turn will lead to increased revenue for the producers of Service B.

23. D: If the price of iPhones goes up, more consumers will either buy other phones or go without a phone. This is reflected in the downward slope of the demand curve.

24. E: Demand for an inferior good decreases when income goes up, while demand for a normal good increases as income rises.

25. C: Choice a. yields 50 utils, Choice b. yields 60 utils, Choice c. yields 63 utils, Choice d. yields 60 utils and Choice e. yields 34 utils. Since Kenny is maximizing utility, he should buy 4 of good X and 3 of good Y

26. D: Because Jasmine's income will increase, she will be able to buy some increased combination of good A and good B, and her total utility will increase as a result.

27. B: Because Brittany's demand for good B decreases when her income increases, it is an inferior good. Her demand for good A increases, meaning it is a normal good. And with the increased income, she can purchase more goods, leading to greater total utility from her purchases. We do not know if goods A and B are substitutes or not based on the given information.

28. D: With the increase in the price of good B, and no increase in income, Randy will have to alter his purchasing habits to stay within his budget constraint.

29. C: The law of diminishing marginal utility states that at some point a consumer will notice less satisfaction from a good or service at each consecutive consumption level of that product.

30. E: By definition, production in the short run is the time period during which a plant cannot increase production capacity, and production in the long run is the time period during which production capacity can be changed.

31. A: The input and output data illustrate the Law of Diminishing Marginal Returns, which states that as inputs are added during production, there eventually comes a time when increased inputs coincide with a decrease in marginal return.

32. B: Marginal cost is the additional cost necessary to produce another unit. The total cost to produce the 2nd output is $58, and the total cost to produce the 3rd output is $70. The change in total cost is $12, which is the marginal cost of the 3rd output.

33. A: As the firm moves from producing 0 units to producing 20 units, it experiences economies of scale. Notice that its average total cost for each additional unit decreases as production increases from 0 to 20. This decreased average total cost as quantity produced increases is the definition of economies of scale.

34. C: To determine the least-cost, profit-maximizing combination of inputs, the company should use both inputs to the point where their marginal revenue product is equal to their price.

35. B: For the third labor unit, the marginal product is the increase in production from the second unit to the third ($40 - 30 = 10$) and the marginal revenue product is the increase in revenue from the second unit to the third ($400 - 300 = 100$).

36. D: According to the Law of Diminishing Marginal Returns, marginal product will initially increase as the units of an input are increased, but then the curve will flatten out and eventually the marginal product will begin to decrease.

37. A: The long run average total cost curve of a firm is a curve that connects the minimums from all of the firm's different short run average total cost curves.

38. A: The accounting profit equals revenues minus costs. Economic profit is also concerned with opportunity costs.

39. D: The accounting profit is \$220,000 – \$200,000 = \$20,000; the economic profit (or loss) is \$220,000 – \$200,000 – \$40,000 = (–\$20,000); and the opportunity cost of starting the new business equals \$40,000 because that was the "opportunity cost" of the next-best forgone opportunity.

40. C: In a perfectly competitive market, firms will operate where MR = MC.

41. A: In a perfectly competitive market, a firm is experiencing a short run loss if its total costs are greater than total revenue. A firm should still continue producing in the short run even if losing money provided that the total revenue is greater than the total variable costs.

42. D: In the short run, a perfectly competitive firm should shut down if total costs exceed total revenue and if the total variable costs exceed total revenue. If total revenue exceeds total variable costs, the firm should continue production. The difference between total revenue and total fixed costs is not part of this determination.

43. E: For a perfectly competitive firm, efficiency is reached when marginal costs equal marginal revenue and where price = marginal costs. While this is the point at which profit is maximized for a perfectly competitive firm, maximum profit does not equal price. In a perfectly competitive firm profit is \$0. Since the price is some value greater than \$0, it can be shown maximum profit does not equal price.

44. B: A monopolist produces at price above the minimum ATC, unlike a firm in perfect competition, and at an output below the intersection of the demand and marginal cost curves.

45. D: A monopoly creates inefficiencies by producing at a higher price than a perfectly competitive firm and by producing fewer goods than a perfectly competitive firm would. A monopoly also produces where MR = MC, which is where a perfectly competitive firm produces, however the monopoly will set price where that output level intersects the demand curve.

46. B: If the firms in an oligopoly create a cartel, they will increase prices and lower productions when compared to the standards of a perfectly competitive firm in an attempt to increase profit.

47. C: The firms in an oligopoly may collude intentionally or unintentionally. The rest of the options are wrong: an oligopoly has many barriers to entry, including great economies of scale. This creates a "kinked" demand curve. Because of the barriers to entry, an oligopoly has few firms, not many.

48. E: Firms in a monopolistic competition are not efficient. They earn a profit above the minimum ATC, meaning they are not efficient productively, and they create output at a level less than the level of allocative efficiency.

49. C: If Ciao Bella hires another worker, the MRC will be greater than the MRP. This will lead to a further decrease in profits.

50. A: Perfect competition is a theoretical type of market more so than one actually found in real life. That's because it is the most efficient, operating where P = MR = MC.

51. B: Monopolies, like firms in all market structures, attempt to maximize profits. However, because competition is limited, they are able to set a price above marginal costs, leading to an inefficient utilization of resources.

52. E: A market that is monopolistically competitive is relatively easy to enter and exit and has high levels of competition. Therefore, firms will enter and exit the market if it is not in long-run equilibrium. When price/quantity is below the minimum of the average total cost curve firms will exit the market.

53. D: In the short run, Bob's should continue to operate even if total revenues are less than total costs provide total revenues are at least greater than total variable costs. This means that the variable costs of operating would be covered and at least some of the fixed costs would be covered. In Bob's case, however, total variable costs are not covered, and so Bob's should shut down instead of incurring greater expenses by continuing to operate.

54. D: Firms are attracted by an economic profit, where MR is greater than MC, and will enter a market until a normal profit returns, where MR = MC.

55. A: The marginal product of labor of the fifth worker hired is 2, the total output for 4 workers subtracted from the total output for 5 workers.

56. A: Because oil transport is a derived factor of oil sales, when oil demand increases, oil transport demand will increase along with it.

57. E: All options listed are derived factors, because their demand originates from the demand for the good or service they are used to make.

58. C: The Lorenz Curve is a graph used to represent the distribution of income in a population. A straight 45 degree line represents a perfectly equal distribution of income.

59. C: Firms in perfect competition are price takers. Their MRP = [marginal physical product] × [price], and their demand curve is horizontal. Firms in monopolistic competition, however, face a downward-sloping demand curve: they must lower their prices to sell additional units.

60. C: Firms hire to the point where marginal revenue product (MRP) equals marginal cost (MC) but will not hire when MRP is lower than MC. Because MRP is determined by multiplying price by the marginal physical product (MPP), in this case the MRP is $100, which is less than the MC of $110. The firm will not hire the worker because it would cause additional losses, but there is not enough information to suggest the firm would lay off other workers or shut down.

61. C: A monopsonist faces an upward-sloping supply curve for labor, not a downward-sloping curve. The rest of the statements are all true.

62. C: A labor union reduces the supply of labor, thereby raising the wage rate above the equilibrium wage rate that would be earned in a perfectly competitive labor market. The supply curve for labor shifts to the left when a labor market is unionized.

63. E: When the minimum wage is set above the equilibrium wage rate for the market, supply for the labor will increase and demand will decrease. The initial effect of this the decreased demand will be an increase in unemployment. The shrinking labor force will later bring about a decrease in unemployment, though it's not clear from the information how large that will be.

64. D: Felt and hat-making labor are derived factors for men's hats. If the price of men's hat decreases, demand for the hats will increase. That means demand for factors used to make men's hats will also increase, as will the price of those factors.

65. A: In a competitive labor market, the wage rate is set where the supply curve for labor intersects MRP.

66. D: If a new, higher minimum wage is set, employers will be willing to employ fewer workers at the higher wage.

67. B: The benefit to the company is known as a private benefit. The benefit to the neighborhood is known as the external benefit. Social benefits are the total of private benefits and external benefits.

68. E: Costs of a good borne by society include the cost to pay for the product ($100 in this case), known as the private cost; the indirect costs borne by society (unwanted pollution in this case), known as the external cost; and social costs, the total of private costs and external costs.

69. C: The impact of a transaction on third parties not involved in the transaction is known as an externality. An externality can be positive, in which case it's a positive externality or social benefit. An externality can also be negative, in which case it's a negative externality or a social cost.

70. B: By definition, a public good is a good that users cannot be required to pay for even if they use the good. This is called non-excludable. A public good is also non-rivalrous, meaning the use of the good does not prevent another user from using the same good.

71. E: By definition, I and II are correct: a public good is non-excludable and non-rivalrous. In addition, because users do not pay for public goods, it is difficult to determine how much a user values the good.

72. C: As a result of the increased quality regulation, production costs for televisions will increase, and producers will pass along those additional costs in the form of higher prices for televisions. The higher prices will cause a reduction in demand.

73. C: Statements A, B, D, and E are all correct. However, if the government imposes a tax on a good with a highly inelastic demand, producers can shift a lot of the cost of the tax onto consumers, since demand does not vary much as price increases.

74. D: By definition, a public good is one that is non-excludable and non-rivalrous. The non-excludable nature of a public good is stated by option D.

75. B: Because the perceived value of a clean environment increases, the marginal benefit curve for anti-pollution technologies that help keep an environment clean will shift to the right. This will provide incentive to firms to supply more anti-pollution technologies, as the market will now pay more for those technologies but will not shift the supply or MC curves.

76. D: If a society wants greater income equity, it will impose a progressive income tax, which taxes the wealthy at a higher rate; an inheritance tax, which prevents the wealthy from passing all their wealth on to the next generation; and a gift tax, which prevents the wealthy from simply giving their wealth away.

77. B: A sales tax of 8% is a regressive tax, because it takes a higher percentage of a poor person's income to pay the tax than it does of a rich person's income.

78. E: A market failure is any situation in which the production of a good or service is not efficient. In the cases listed, non-competitive markets allow for the underpayment of labor and the underproduction of a good or service; externalities are negative consequences assumed by parties not involved in a transaction; and public goods are an example of a good the market will not produce at all, or at efficient levels.

79. A: Taxes, subsidies, price ceilings, price floors, taxes, and government regulations can all be used to try to correct market failures, in which the market does not produce goods and services efficiently. Societies try to use some or all of these techniques to adjust the market's production of goods and services, including externalities of the goods and services.

80. E: The US federal government plays many roles in the US society. These include regulating industries, such as communication and food production; the imposition of taxes, such as the federal income tax; the provision of programs designed to help poor people who would otherwise suffer more, such as Medicare and Medicaid; and the provision of public goods, including the US military and the National Park system.

How to Overcome Test Anxiety

Just the thought of taking a test is enough to make most people a little nervous. A test is an important event that can have a long-term impact on your future, so it's important to take it seriously and it's natural to feel anxious about performing well. But just because anxiety is normal, that doesn't mean that it's helpful in test taking, or that you should simply accept it as part of your life. Anxiety can have a variety of effects. These effects can be mild, like making you feel slightly nervous, or severe, like blocking your ability to focus or remember even a simple detail.

If you experience test anxiety—whether severe or mild—it's important to know how to beat it. To discover this, first you need to understand what causes test anxiety.

Causes of Test Anxiety

While we often think of anxiety as an uncontrollable emotional state, it can actually be caused by simple, practical things. One of the most common causes of test anxiety is that a person does not feel adequately prepared for their test. This feeling can be the result of many different issues such as poor study habits or lack of organization, but the most common culprit is time management. Starting to study too late, failing to organize your study time to cover all of the material, or being distracted while you study will mean that you're not well prepared for the test. This may lead to cramming the night before, which will cause you to be physically and mentally exhausted for the test. Poor time management also contributes to feelings of stress, fear, and hopelessness as you realize you are not well prepared but don't know what to do about it.

Other times, test anxiety is not related to your preparation for the test but comes from unresolved fear. This may be a past failure on a test, or poor performance on tests in general. It may come from comparing yourself to others who seem to be performing better or from the stress of living up to expectations. Anxiety may be driven by fears of the future—how failure on this test would affect your educational and career goals. These fears are often completely irrational, but they can still negatively impact your test performance.

Elements of Test Anxiety

As mentioned earlier, test anxiety is considered to be an emotional state, but it has physical and mental components as well. Sometimes you may not even realize that you are suffering from test anxiety until you notice the physical symptoms. These can include trembling hands, rapid heartbeat, sweating, nausea, and tense muscles. Extreme anxiety may lead to fainting or vomiting. Obviously, any of these symptoms can have a negative impact on testing. It is important to recognize them as soon as they begin to occur so that you can address the problem before it damages your performance.

The mental components of test anxiety include trouble focusing and inability to remember learned information. During a test, your mind is on high alert, which can help you recall information and stay focused for an extended period of time. However, anxiety interferes with your mind's natural processes, causing you to blank out, even on the questions you know well. The strain of testing during anxiety makes it difficult to stay focused, especially on a test that may take several hours. Extreme anxiety can take a huge mental toll, making it difficult not only to recall test information but even to understand the test questions or pull your thoughts together.

Effects of Test Anxiety

Test anxiety is like a disease—if left untreated, it will get progressively worse. Anxiety leads to poor performance, and this reinforces the feelings of fear and failure, which in turn lead to poor performances on subsequent tests. It can grow from a mild nervousness to a crippling condition. If allowed to progress, test anxiety can have a big impact on your schooling, and consequently on your future.

Test anxiety can spread to other parts of your life. Anxiety on tests can become anxiety in any stressful situation, and blanking on a test can turn into panicking in a job situation. But fortunately, you don't have to let anxiety rule your testing and determine your grades. There are a number of relatively simple steps you can take to move past anxiety and function normally on a test and in the rest of life.

Physical Steps for Beating Test Anxiety

While test anxiety is a serious problem, the good news is that it can be overcome. It doesn't have to control your ability to think and remember information. While it may take time, you can begin taking steps today to beat anxiety.

Just as your first hint that you may be struggling with anxiety comes from the physical symptoms, the first step to treating it is also physical. Rest is crucial for having a clear, strong mind. If you are tired, it is much easier to give in to anxiety. But if you establish good sleep habits, your body and mind will be ready to perform optimally, without the strain of exhaustion. Additionally, sleeping well helps you to retain information better, so you're more likely to recall the answers when you see the test questions.

Getting good sleep means more than going to bed on time. It's important to allow your brain time to relax. Take study breaks from time to time so it doesn't get overworked, and don't study right before bed. Take time to rest your mind before trying to rest your body, or you may find it difficult to fall asleep.

Along with sleep, other aspects of physical health are important in preparing for a test. Good nutrition is vital for good brain function. Sugary foods and drinks may give a burst of energy but this burst is followed by a crash, both physically and emotionally. Instead, fuel your body with protein and vitamin-rich foods.

Also, drink plenty of water. Dehydration can lead to headaches and exhaustion, especially if your brain is already under stress from the rigors of the test. Particularly if your test is a long one, drink water during the breaks. And if possible, take an energy-boosting snack to eat between sections.

Along with sleep and diet, a third important part of physical health is exercise. Maintaining a steady workout schedule is helpful, but even taking 5-minute study breaks to walk can help get your blood pumping faster and clear your head. Exercise also releases endorphins, which contribute to a positive feeling and can help combat test anxiety.

When you nurture your physical health, you are also contributing to your mental health. If your body is healthy, your mind is much more likely to be healthy as well. So take time to rest, nourish your body with healthy food and water, and get moving as much as possible. Taking these physical steps will make you stronger and more able to take the mental steps necessary to overcome test anxiety.

Mental Steps for Beating Test Anxiety

Working on the mental side of test anxiety can be more challenging, but as with the physical side, there are clear steps you can take to overcome it. As mentioned earlier, test anxiety often stems from lack of preparation, so the obvious solution is to prepare for the test. Effective studying may be the most important weapon you have for beating test anxiety, but you can and should employ several other mental tools to combat fear.

First, boost your confidence by reminding yourself of past success—tests or projects that you aced. If you're putting as much effort into preparing for this test as you did for those, there's no reason you should expect to fail here. Work hard to prepare; then trust your preparation.

Second, surround yourself with encouraging people. It can be helpful to find a study group, but be sure that the people you're around will encourage a positive attitude. If you spend time with others who are anxious or cynical, this will only contribute to your own anxiety. Look for others who are motivated to study hard from a desire to succeed, not from a fear of failure.

Third, reward yourself. A test is physically and mentally tiring, even without anxiety, and it can be helpful to have something to look forward to. Plan an activity following the test, regardless of the outcome, such as going to a movie or getting ice cream.

When you are taking the test, if you find yourself beginning to feel anxious, remind yourself that you know the material. Visualize successfully completing the test. Then take a few deep, relaxing breaths and return to it. Work through the questions carefully but with confidence, knowing that you are capable of succeeding.

Developing a healthy mental approach to test taking will also aid in other areas of life. Test anxiety affects more than just the actual test—it can be damaging to your mental health and even contribute to depression. It's important to beat test anxiety before it becomes a problem for more than testing.

Study Strategy

Being prepared for the test is necessary to combat anxiety, but what does being prepared look like? You may study for hours on end and still not feel prepared. What you need is a strategy for test prep. The next few pages outline our recommended steps to help you plan out and conquer the challenge of preparation.

Step 1: Scope Out the Test

Learn everything you can about the format (multiple choice, essay, etc.) and what will be on the test. Gather any study materials, course outlines, or sample exams that may be available. Not only will this help you to prepare, but knowing what to expect can help to alleviate test anxiety.

Step 2: Map Out the Material

Look through the textbook or study guide and make note of how many chapters or sections it has. Then divide these over the time you have. For example, if a book has 15 chapters and you have five days to study, you need to cover three chapters each day. Even better, if you have the time, leave an extra day at the end for overall review after you have gone through the material in depth.

If time is limited, you may need to prioritize the material. Look through it and make note of which sections you think you already have a good grasp on, and which need review. While you are studying, skim quickly through the familiar sections and take more time on the challenging parts.

Write out your plan so you don't get lost as you go. Having a written plan also helps you feel more in control of the study, so anxiety is less likely to arise from feeling overwhelmed at the amount to cover.

Step 3: Gather Your Tools

Decide what study method works best for you. Do you prefer to highlight in the book as you study and then go back over the highlighted portions? Or do you type out notes of the important information? Or is it helpful to make flashcards that you can carry with you? Assemble the pens, index cards, highlighters, post-it notes, and any other materials you may need so you won't be distracted by getting up to find things while you study.

If you're having a hard time retaining the information or organizing your notes, experiment with different methods. For example, try color-coding by subject with colored pens, highlighters, or post-it notes. If you learn better by hearing, try recording yourself reading your notes so you can listen while in the car, working out, or simply sitting at your desk. Ask a friend to quiz you from your flashcards, or try teaching someone the material to solidify it in your mind.

Step 4: Create Your Environment

It's important to avoid distractions while you study. This includes both the obvious distractions like visitors and the subtle distractions like an uncomfortable chair (or a too-comfortable couch that makes you want to fall asleep). Set up the best study environment possible: good lighting and a comfortable work area. If background music helps you focus, you may want to turn it on, but otherwise keep the room quiet. If you are using a computer to take notes, be sure you don't have any other windows open, especially applications like social media, games, or anything else that could distract you. Silence your phone and turn off notifications. Be sure to keep water close by so you stay hydrated while you study (but avoid unhealthy drinks and snacks).

Also, take into account the best time of day to study. Are you freshest first thing in the morning? Try to set aside some time then to work through the material. Is your mind clearer in the afternoon or evening? Schedule your study session then. Another method is to study at the same time of day that you will take the test, so that your brain gets used to working on the material at that time and will be ready to focus at test time.

Step 5: Study!

Once you have done all the study preparation, it's time to settle into the actual studying. Sit down, take a few moments to settle your mind so you can focus, and begin to follow your study plan. Don't give in to distractions or let yourself procrastinate. This is your time to prepare so you'll be ready to fearlessly approach the test. Make the most of the time and stay focused.

Of course, you don't want to burn out. If you study too long you may find that you're not retaining the information very well. Take regular study breaks. For example, taking five minutes out of every hour to walk briskly, breathing deeply and swinging your arms, can help your mind stay fresh.

As you get to the end of each chapter or section, it's a good idea to do a quick review. Remind yourself of what you learned and work on any difficult parts. When you feel that you've mastered the material, move on to the next part. At the end of your study session, briefly skim through your notes again.

But while review is helpful, cramming last minute is NOT. If at all possible, work ahead so that you won't need to fit all your study into the last day. Cramming overloads your brain with more information than it can process and retain, and your tired mind may struggle to recall even previously learned information when it is overwhelmed with last-minute study. Also, the urgent nature of cramming and the stress placed on your brain contribute to anxiety. You'll be more likely to go to the test feeling unprepared and having trouble thinking clearly.

So don't cram, and don't stay up late before the test, even just to review your notes at a leisurely pace. Your brain needs rest more than it needs to go over the information again. In fact, plan to finish your studies by noon or early afternoon the day before the test. Give your brain the rest of the day to relax or focus on other things, and get a good night's sleep. Then you will be fresh for the test and better able to recall what you've studied.

Step 6: Take a Practice Test

Many courses offer sample tests, either online or in the study materials. This is an excellent resource to check whether you have mastered the material, as well as to prepare for the test format and environment.

Check the test format ahead of time: the number of questions, the type (multiple choice, free response, etc.), and the time limit. Then create a plan for working through them. For example, if you have 30 minutes to take a 60-question test, your limit is 30 seconds per question. Spend less time on the questions you know well so that you can take more time on the difficult ones.

If you have time to take several practice tests, take the first one open book, with no time limit. Work through the questions at your own pace and make sure you fully understand them. Gradually work up to taking a test under test conditions: sit at a desk with all study materials put away and set a timer. Pace yourself to make sure you finish the test with time to spare and go back to check your answers if you have time.

After each test, check your answers. On the questions you missed, be sure you understand why you missed them. Did you misread the question (tests can use tricky wording)? Did you forget the information? Or was it something you hadn't learned? Go back and study any shaky areas that the practice tests reveal.

Taking these tests not only helps with your grade, but also aids in combating test anxiety. If you're already used to the test conditions, you're less likely to worry about it, and working through tests until you're scoring well gives you a confidence boost. Go through the practice tests until you feel comfortable, and then you can go into the test knowing that you're ready for it.

Test Tips

On test day, you should be confident, knowing that you've prepared well and are ready to answer the questions. But aside from preparation, there are several test day strategies you can employ to maximize your performance.

First, as stated before, get a good night's sleep the night before the test (and for several nights before that, if possible). Go into the test with a fresh, alert mind rather than staying up late to study.

Try not to change too much about your normal routine on the day of the test. It's important to eat a nutritious breakfast, but if you normally don't eat breakfast at all, consider eating just a protein bar. If you're a coffee drinker, go ahead and have your normal coffee. Just make sure you time it so that the caffeine doesn't wear off right in the middle of your test. Avoid sugary beverages, and drink enough water to stay hydrated but not so much that you need a restroom break 10 minutes into the test. If your test isn't first thing in the morning, consider going for a walk or doing a light workout before the test to get your blood flowing.

Allow yourself enough time to get ready, and leave for the test with plenty of time to spare so you won't have the anxiety of scrambling to arrive in time. Another reason to be early is to select a good seat. It's helpful to sit away from doors and windows, which can be distracting. Find a good seat, get out your supplies, and settle your mind before the test begins.

When the test begins, start by going over the instructions carefully, even if you already know what to expect. Make sure you avoid any careless mistakes by following the directions.

Then begin working through the questions, pacing yourself as you've practiced. If you're not sure on an answer, don't spend too much time on it, and don't let it shake your confidence. Either skip it and come back later, or eliminate as many wrong answers as possible and guess among the remaining ones. Don't dwell on these questions as you continue—put them out of your mind and focus on what lies ahead.

Be sure to read all of the answer choices, even if you're sure the first one is the right answer. Sometimes you'll find a better one if you keep reading. But don't second-guess yourself if you do immediately know the answer. Your gut instinct is usually right. Don't let test anxiety rob you of the information you know.

If you have time at the end of the test (and if the test format allows), go back and review your answers. Be cautious about changing any, since your first instinct tends to be correct, but make sure you didn't misread any of the questions or accidentally mark the wrong answer choice. Look over any you skipped and make an educated guess.

At the end, leave the test feeling confident. You've done your best, so don't waste time worrying about your performance or wishing you could change anything. Instead, celebrate the successful completion of this test. And finally, use this test to learn how to deal with anxiety even better next time.

Review Video: Test Anxiety
Visit mometrix.com/academy and enter code: 100340

Important Qualification

Not all anxiety is created equal. If your test anxiety is causing major issues in your life beyond the classroom or testing center, or if you are experiencing troubling physical symptoms related to your anxiety, it may be a sign of a serious physiological or psychological condition. If this sounds like your situation, we strongly encourage you to seek professional help.

Online Resources

Due to our efforts to try to keep this book to a manageable length, we've created a link that will give you access to all of your online resources:

mometrix.com/resources719/apmicroeconom

It's Your Moment, Let's Celebrate It!

Share your story @mometrixtestpreparation